ESSENTI

MADRID

★ Best places to see 34–55

■ Featured sight

■ Around Old Madrid 81–112

■ Eastern Madrid 113–128

■ Northern Madrid 129–155

Original text by Paul Wade and Kathy Arnold
Updated by Paul Wade and Kathy Arnold

© Automobile Association Developments Limited 2008
First published 2008

ISBN 978-0-7495-5364-7

Published by AA Publishing, a trading name of Automobile Association Developments Limited, whose registered office is Fanum House, Basing View, Basingstoke, Hampshire RG21 4EA.
Registered number 1878835.

Automobile Association Developments Limited retains the copyright in the original edition © 2000 and in all subsequent editions, reprints and amendments

A CIP catalogue record for this book is available from the British Library

All rights reserved. No part of this publication may be reproduced, stored in a retrieval system, or transmitted in any form or by any means – electronic, photocopying, recording or otherwise – unless the written permission of the publishers has been obtained beforehand. This book may not be sold, resold, hired out or otherwise disposed of by way of trade in any form of binding or cover other than that in which it is published, without the prior consent of the publisher. The contents of this publication are believed correct at the time of printing. Nevertheless, AA Publishing accept no responsibility for errors, omissions or changes in the details given, or for the consequences of readers' reliance on this information. This does not affect your statutory rights. Assessments of attractions, hotels and restaurants are based upon the author's own experience and contain subjective opinions that may not reflect the publisher's opinion or a reader's experience. We have tried to ensure accuracy, but things do change, so please let us know if you have any comments or corrections.

Colour separation: MRM Graphics Ltd
Printed and bound in Italy by Printer Trento S.r.l.

A03164
Maps in this title produced from:
    mapping © MAIRDUMONT / Falk Verlag 2007
    mapping © ISTITUTO GEOGRAFICO DE AGOSTINI S.p.A., NOVARA 2006
Transport map © Communicarta Ltd, UK

About this book

Symbols are used to denote the following categories:

- ✚ map reference to maps on cover
- ✉ address or location
- ☎ telephone number
- 🕒 opening times
- 👆 admission charge
- 🍴 restaurant or café on premises or nearby
- Ⓜ nearest underground train station
- 🚌 nearest bus/tram route
- 🚆 nearest overground train station
- ⛴ nearest ferry stop
- ✈ nearest airport
- ❓ other practical information
- ℹ tourist information office
- ► indicates the page where you will find a fuller description

This book is divided into six sections.
The essence of Madrid pages 6–19
Introduction; Features; Food and Drink; Short Break including the 10 Essentials

Planning pages 20–33
Before You Go; Getting There; Getting Around; Being There

Best places to see pages 34–55
The unmissable highlights of any visit to Madrid

Best things to do pages 56–77
Great cafés; stunning views; places to take the children and more

Exploring pages 78–155
The best places to visit in Madrid, organized by area

Excursions pages 156–181
Places to visit out of town

Maps
All map references are to the maps on the covers. For example, the Museo del Prado has the reference ✚ 20K – indicating the grid square in which it is to be found

Admission prices
Inexpensive (under €6)
Moderate (€6–€10)
Expensive (over €10)

Hotel prices
Prices are per double room per night:
€ budget (under €100); €€ moderate (€100–€150); €€€ expensive (over €150)

Restaurant prices
Prices are for a three-course meal per person without drinks:
€ budget (under €15); €€ moderate (€15–€30); €€€ expensive (€30)

Contents

THE ESSENCE OF...

6 – 19

PLANNING

20 – 33

BEST PLACES TO SEE

34 – 55

BEST THINGS TO DO

56 – 77

EXPLORING...

78 – 155

EXCURSIONS

156 – 181

The essence of...

Introduction	8–9
Features	10–11
Food and Drink	12–15
Short Break	16–19

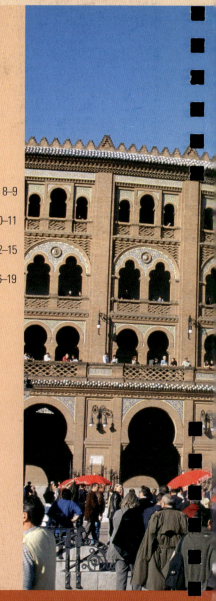

THE ESSENCE OF MADRID

THE ESSENCE OF MADRID

Madrid is one of the world's great capital cities, with inhabitants who are intensely proud of their traditions. They order *cocido madrileño* (a classic Madrid stew), stroll in the Retiro Park on a Sunday morning and dance the *chotis* in the street during the festival of San Isidro. Most of all they love to stay up late, eating dinner at 11, and chatting in the *terrazas* (open-air cafés) until dawn. While the days are devoted to boring essentials such as working, Madrid really comes to life at night – if you can't beat 'em, join 'em.

THE ESSENCE OF MADRID

features

Madrid was the capital of the world's first intercontinental empire. Between the 16th and 19th centuries, Spain ruled South, Central and much of North America, with colonies as far afield as the Philippines. No wonder every church seems more ornate than the last, and museums abound, crammed with masterpieces. The palaces are grand, ministries forbidding and houses enormous. When it comes to sheer grandeur, Madrid stands shoulder to shoulder with London, Paris and Rome.

The city has many faces. We enjoy exploring the medieval clutter of streets that scuttle away from the Plaza Mayor, down to the rabbit warren of La Latina and Lavapiés. Then there is the Habsburg quarter, west of the Puerta del Sol, and the high-class, trendy area of the *paseos* (boulevards) and Calle de Serrano. Walking around the city is a pleasure, but you can also hop on the Metro, the cheap, efficient underground system linking every spot you will ever want to visit.

GEOGRAPHY

Madrid, the capital of Spain, is in the centre of the Iberian peninsula. Standing on a plateau some

650m (2,130ft) above sea level, it is about 550–600km (340–370 miles) from both the Atlantic Ocean and the Mediterranean.

THE ESSENCE OF MADRID

CLIMATE
A Spanish saying describes Madrid as having nine months of winter and three months of hell. Certainly, winters are cold, with occasional snow, while summers are hot, with temperatures often over 35°C (95°F). Overall, the air is dry, with an annual average of 2,730 hours of sunshine. Spring and autumn are the best times of year to visit, with warm days and cool nights.

PEOPLE AND ECONOMY
Over five million live in the province of Madrid, with three million in the city itself. Many come from other parts of Spain, as well as former Spanish colonies such as Argentina, Mexico and Ecuador.

LEISURE FACILITIES
Madrid has at least 40 significant museums. Many are undergoing a much-needed upgrading to improve presentation and enjoyment by non-Spanish-speaking visitors. Few cities can rival the three jewels in Madrid's crown: the Museo del Prado (the Prado), the Museo Nacional Centro de Arte Reina Sofía and the Museo Thyssen-Bornemisza.

In addition to cultural centres there are also amusement parks, swimming pools, a zoo and more than 4,000 restaurants.

PROVINCE OF MADRID
The metropolis is also the chief city of the province of Madrid, which encompasses 8,000sq km (3,090sq miles) and includes cities such as Alcalá de Henares and Aranjuez. Just 52km (32 miles) to the north, the Sierra de Guadarrama provides skiing in the winter. Government and banking provide jobs in the city, and there are textile, food and metal-working industries in the surrounding area.

THE ESSENCE OF MADRID

food & drink

***Madrileños* are a sociable people for whom eating and drinking in bars and restaurants is a way of life. They tend to enjoy traditional dishes made from fresh, full-flavoured ingredients, often prepared quite simply.**

Try Madrid-style cooking, then sample the cuisines from all the regions of Spain, from the Basque country to Galicia, and from Asturias to Valencia. Portions are usually hearty and prices reasonable.

The city also boasts world-class chefs, such as Sergi Arola at La Broche and Santi Santamaria i Puig at Santceloni.

Desserts, however, tend to be standard and unadventurous. They include the ubiquitous *flan* (crème caramel), *arroz con leche* (rice pudding) and *manzana asada* (baked apple).

FISH AND MEAT DISHES
Madrid is often called Spain's main fishing port because the fleets send the best of their catch straight to the city. Sauces are rarely needed for the thick slices of *lubina* (John Dory), *besugo* (sea bass)

THE ESSENCE OF MADRID

and *ventresca* (tuna), which are grilled *a la plancha* (on a hot plate). Basque restaurants are particularly well known for their fish dishes, which have relatively simple sauces, such as white wine with garlic and parsley. The Spanish are also great meat eaters, choosing between tender pork, *chuletas de lechal* (lamb chops) and chunks of *solomillo* (sirloin steak). There is also a vast array of sausages, from *chorizos* (spicy pork) to *morcilla* (black pudding).

Madrid's own dish is *cocido madrileño*, a stew of meat and vegetables that traditionally is prepared in an earthenware pot by the fire. Lamb and suckling pig are roasted slowly in wood-fired ovens, until the meat is so tender that it falls off the bone.

SNACKS

Don't miss *tapas*, the little snacks that are eaten throughout the day, but especially in the late afternoon and early evening before restaurants open for dinner. A *tapa* was once a small round slice of bread set on top of your wine glass – a simple device to stop flies crawling in! Someone added a slice of ham, an olive or a marinated

13

THE ESSENCE OF MADRID

pepper and – hey presto! – the *tapa* was born. An automatic companion to a small glass of wine, they range from slices of cheese or sausage to meatballs or snails. Every bar has its own speciality.

Another must is *chocolate con churros*, which are popular at breakfast or teatime. Cups of hot, thick drinking chocolate traditionally come with

THE ESSENCE OF MADRID

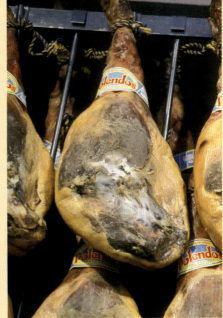

churros. Variously translated as doughnuts or fritters, these are light, crispy, deep-fried batter, shaped in Madrid-style teardrops, or in long, thick sticks, called *porras*. Dip them in sugar, or better still, dunk them in your hot chocolate.

WINE

Spain is rich in vineyards, but in recent years there has been a renaissance in wine-making in the province of Madrid. Look for wines labelled D O Vinos de Madrid. Among the *blancos* (whites) try Albillo, Tapón de Oro and Viña Bayona. Good *rosados* (rosés) are Tapón de Oro, Valfrío and Puerta del Sol, while reliable *tintos* (reds) include Valdeguerra and Tochuelo Tinto.

THE ESSENCE OF MADRID

short break

If you only have a short time to visit Madrid and would like to take home some unforgettable memories, you can do something local and capture the real flavour of the city. The following suggestions will give you a wide range of sights and experiences that won't take long, won't cost very much and will make your visit very special.

● **Buy the special *Abono Paseo del Arte* ticket and visit all three great art galleries:** the Prado (➤ 44–45), the Museo Nacional Centro de Arte Reina Sofía (➤ 42–43) and the Museo Thyssen-Bornemisza (➤ 48–49).

● **Do what *madrileños* do on Sunday morning:** wander among the stamp and coin stalls on the Plaza Mayor (➤ 54–55); search for a bargain in the Rastro flea market (➤ 66, 102); or stroll through the Retiro Park (➤ 52–53).

THE ESSENCE OF MADRID

THE ESSENCE OF MADRID

- **Sit out at a *terraza*** (an open-air café), along the Paseo de la Castellana until 2 in the morning.

- **Drink a *fino* sherry** at La Venencia (➤ 65) or a vermouth with soda at Casa Alberto (➤ 69).

- **Order a *cocido madrileño*** (a classic Madrid stew), cooked in an earthenware pot by the fire at La Posada de la Villa (➤ 98).

- **Go shopping,** or window shopping, on Calle de Serrano (➤ 130) to see how the other half spends its money.

THE ESSENCE OF MADRID

- **Go and watch a football match** at Real Madrid's Bernabéu Stadium (➤ 134), or at the Vicente Calderón stadium, home of rival Atlético Madrid.

- **Take a siesta;** it's probably the only way you can stay up late.

- **Sip hot chocolate** and eat *churros* (like doughnuts) at the Chocolatería San Ginés (➤ 64).

- **Tour the Palacio Real,** the monumental royal palace (➤ 50–51).

Planning

Before you go	22–25
Getting there	26
Getting around	27–29
Being there	30–33

PLANNING

Before you go

WHEN TO GO

Spring, early summer and autumn are the best times to visit Madrid. The days are warm, the evenings are cool: just right for exploring the city's narrow lanes and old streets. However, there is a Spanish saying, describing the capital's climate as: *nueve meses de invierno, tres meses de infierno*. Don't be put off by the translation: nine months of winter, three months of hell.

It can get bitterly cold in winter, especially when the wind gets up, with temperatures rarely above freezing during the day. But it is warm on the Metro, warm in the museums and very cheerful in the bars. By contrast, high summer can be very hot indeed. So go with the flow: have a siesta in the afternoon and stay up late.

WHAT YOU NEED

- ● Required
- ○ Suggested
- ▲ Not required

Some countries require a passport to remain valid for a minimum period (usually at least six months) beyond the date of entry – check before you travel.

	UK	Germany	USA	Netherlands
Passport (or National Identity Card where applicable)	●	●	●	●
Visa (regulations can change – check before you travel)	▲	▲	▲	▲
Onward or Return Ticket	▲	▲	▲	▲
Health Inoculations (tetanus and polio)	▲	▲	●	▲
Health Documentation (► 23, Health Insurance)	●	●	●	●
Travel Insurance	○	○	○	○
Driving Licence (national)	●	●	●	●
Car Insurance Certificate	●	●	●	●
Car Registration Document	●	●	●	●

BEFORE YOU GO

WEBSITES
www.esmadrid.com

www.turismomadrid.es

TOURIST OFFICES AT HOME
In the UK
Spanish Tourist Office
79 New Cavendish Street
London, W1W 6XB
☎ 020 7486 8077; www.spain.info

In the USA
Tourist Office of Spain

666 Fifth Avenue (35th Floor)
New York, NY 10103
☎ 212/265-8822; www.okspain.org
and
8383 Wilshire Boulevard
Suite 960, Beverley Hills
CA 90211
☎ 213/658-7195; www.okspain.org

HEALTH INSURANCE
EU residents carrying the relevant documentation – an EHIC (European Health Insurance Card) – are entitled to free medical treatment and prescribed medicines in Spain. Non-EU citizens are charged private hospital rates, so insurance is essential. English-speaking doctors are available at the Anglo-American Medical Unit ☎ 91 435 18 23.

ADVANCE PASSENGER INFORMATION (API)
Passengers on all flights to and from Spain now have to supply advance passenger information to the Spanish authorities – full given names, surname, nationality, date of birth and travel document details, namely a passport number. Some airports may have a self-service kiosk for this, otherwise staff at check-in desks will be able to collect the information.

TIME DIFFERENCES

GMT 12 noon	Madrid 1PM	Germany 1PM	USA (NY) 7AM	Netherlands 1PM	France 1PM

Madrid is on CET (Central European Time), one hour ahead of GMT (Greenwich Mean Time). Summer time starts on the last Sunday in March and ends on the last Sunday of October.

PLANNING

NATIONAL HOLIDAYS

1 Jan *Año Nuevo* (New Year's Day)
6 Jan *Reyes* (Three Kings)
Mar/Apr *Jueves Santo, Viernes Santo* (Easter Thursday, Good Friday)
1 May *Fiesta del Trabajo* (May Day)
2 May *Día de la Comunidad* (Madrid Day)
15 May *San Isidro* (Madrid's patron saint)
15 Aug *Virgen de la Paloma* (Assumption)
12 Oct *Día de la Hispanidad* (National Day)
1 Nov *Todos los Santos* (All Saints' Day)
9 Nov *Virgen de la Almudena*
6 Dec *Día de la Constitución* (Constitution Day)
8 Dec *La Inmaculada* (Immaculate Conception)
25 Dec *Navidad* (Christmas)

WHAT'S ON WHEN

January *Cabalgata de los Reyes Magos* (5 Jan): the evening procession of the Three Kings leads on to the next day's *Epifania* (Epiphany), when the kings throw sweets to children lining the streets.

February ARCO (Feb): Contemporary Art Fair, a leading event for top artists, dealers and collectors from all over the world, although it is less successful now than it has been in the past.

Carnaval: before Lent, Madrid parties. A ceremony called the *Entierro de la Sardina* (the Burial of the Sardine), takes place in the Casa de Campo (➤ 76–77).

March/April *Semana Santa* (Holy Week): celebrated with solemn processions of penitents through the streets.

May *Dos de Mayo* (2 May): Madrid remembers the day when *madrileños* rose up against the French in 1808.

Festimad (early May): once an 'alternative' festival but now big business right across the spectrum – films, poetry readings, music, dance and more in the Bellas Artes building and in Móstoles, in the suburbs.

San Isidro (15 May): Madrid's patron saint.

Feria del Libro (the Festival of the Book): held in the Parque del Retiro where booksellers set up hundreds of stalls.

June *San Antonio de la Florida* (13 Jun): At the Ermita de San Antonio de la Florída, unmarried girls visit the chapel to make them lucky in love (➤ 132).

San Juan (17–24 Jun): fireworks in the Parque del Retiro to celebrate the festival of St John.

BEFORE YOU GO

Los Veranos de la Villa (Jun–Sep): a season of music, theatre, *zarzuela* (light opera), dance and open-air cinema, put on under the auspices of the Villa de Madrid; the main venue is the Conde-Duque cultural centre.

July *Virgen del Carmen* (16 Jul): local festivals for the Virgin in the suburbs of Chamberí, Villaverde and Vallecas.

August *San Cayetano* (7 Aug), *San Lorenzo* (10 Aug), the *Virgen de la Paloma* (15 Aug): local *fiestas* in La Latina, Argumosa and Lavapiés.

October/November *Festival de Otoño*: a festival involving all the performing arts based around a theme, for example a country or literary figure.

November *Fiesta de la Almudena* (9 Nov): festival of the (female) patron saint of Madrid.

December *Feria de Artesania* (Dec–6 Jan): Advent craft fair centred on the Paseo de Recoletos (➤ 120,121). *Nochevieja* (New Year's Eve): thousands of people fill the Puerta del Sol to watch the clock and follow the tradition of swallowing one grape at each of the 12 strokes of midnight.

PLANNING

Getting there

BY AIR

Aeropuerto de Barajas

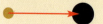

12km (7.5 miles) to city centre

🚈 30 minutes
🚌 45 minutes
🚗 25 minutes

Madrid-Barajas Airport, 12km (7.5 miles) northeast of the city, has four terminals. To get in to the city, Terminals T1, T2 and T3 are served by Metro station Aeropuerto (line 8). Trains run from 6am to 1:30am. Used by major international airlines such as Iberia and British Airways, Terminal 4, the newest terminal, regarded as 'The Gateway to Europe' by passengers from Latin America, is linked to the Barajas station (at the end of Line 8) by EMT bus 201, or to the Aeropuerto station with the free AENA (airport) shuttle buses that run between terminals T2, T3 and T4. For more information on arrivals and departures from each terminal, go to www.aena.es ☎ 90 240 47 04.

BY RAIL

RENFE (www.renfe.es), Spain's national rail company, has two main line stations in the city. Trains from northern Europe, France and Barcelona (including the high-speed AVE train) arrive on the north side of the city at Chamartín. Trains running to Portugal and the south of Spain (including the high-speed AVE train) depart from Atocha, close to the city centre. RENFE's UK agents are Spanish Rail (☎ 020 7725 7063, www.spanish-rail.co.uk) or Freedom Rail (☎ 0870 757 9898, www.freedomrail.co.uk).

BY CAR AND BUS

Thanks to the network of motorways, it is easy to get to Madrid by car. The main roads from the French border include the A-8 and A-1 from Bilbao (4 hours), and the A-2 from Barcelona (6 hours).

For long-distance buses, go to Eurolines with 500 destinations in Europe (www.eurolines.com). Long-distance buses terminate their journeys at Estación Sur near the centre of the city (Calle de Méndez Álvaro ☎ 91 468 42 00).

Getting around

PUBLIC TRANSPORT
Internal flights Iberia, the national carrier, has regular flights linking Madrid with other major cities in Spain. The most frequent are between Madrid and Barcelona, with the *Puente Aéreo* (shuttle service) operating from 6:45am to 11:55pm.

Trains The main office of RENFE (Spanish National Railways) is at Calle de Alcalá 44. Tickets and information are also available at Barajas Airport and the three main stations. From Atocha, trains are mainly to southern Spain. The AVE high-speed service to Seville leaves from Puerta de Atocha. From Chamartín, trains go to the north, northeast and France. Travellers can get discounts on some trips if they travel on so-called 'blue days', marked on calendars available from any RENFE office. A special card for tourists allows unlimited travel on the system.

PLANNING

Buses Estación Sur de Autobuses, the city's main bus station, is at the corner of Calle Méndez Alvaro and Calle Retama. Near by are the Atocha Railway Station and Méndez Alvaro Metro station. Although buses cover the whole of Madrid, the system is somewhat complicated to understand and it is easier to take the Metro.

Metro The easiest way to get around Madrid, apart from on foot, is by Metro. The 11-line, colour-coded system has stops close to all the major attractions. The direction of the train is shown by the name of the terminus station. Trains run 6am–2am. Fares are inexpensive. If you buy a *bono de diez viajes* (10-ride ticket for Metro or bus), you get a discount.

TAXIS
Official taxis are white with a diagonal red stripe. Look for the *libre* (free) sign behind the windscreen (windshield) or a green light on top of the cab. Fares are reasonable. Make sure the meter is not running when you get in. Travel from the airport costs extra.

GETTING AROUND

DRIVING
- The Spanish drive on the right.
- Seat belts must be worn in front seats and rear seats where fitted.
- Penalties are heavy for driving under the influence of alcohol or drugs. It is compulsory to take drink/drug tests when requested by police. Failure to comply is a serious offence.
- It is illegal to drive while wearing headphones or using hand-held mobile phones.
- Fines for traffic offences are stringent and payment is required on the spot.
- Lead-free fuel *(sin plomo)* is readily available. Other types include *super* (4 star), *normal* (3 star) and *gasoleo* (diesel).
- Drivers must carry two warning triangles, spare bulbs and fuses, a spare wheel and a fluorescent jacket. The towing of motor vehicles is not permitted, except to move a broken-down car out of traffic or to a safe place. Only a breakdown vehicle is allowed to tow a broken-down car.
- Speed limits are as follows:
  On motorways 120kph (74mph)   On main roads 100kph (62mph)
  On minor roads 90kph (56mph)   On urban roads 50kph (31mph)

CAR RENTAL
As usual in large airports, all the major car rental companies are represented at Barajas Airport. They also have offices in the middle of Madrid, but you could choose to rent from a local agency. The minimum age for renting a car is 21.

FARES AND CONCESSIONS
Many museums offer free admission to the general public, or citizens of the EU on certain days, or during certain hours. It is important to have a passport or national identity card if you are going to claim a concession (discount).

Students Many museums offer discounts to students on production of an ISIC (international student identity card.)

Senior citizens and under-18s The over-65s and under-18s can gain free entry to many museums and galleries. Children can get reductions on train travel.

Being there

TOURIST OFFICES

Tourist and Cultural Information Line
☎ 010 (91 366 66 04 outside Madrid)

Oficina Municipal de Turismo
Plaza Mayor 3
☎ 91 366 54 77 or 91 588 16 36

Oficinas de Información Turística de la Communidad de Madrid
Calle Duque de Medinaceli 2
☎ 91 429 49 51

Also at
Mercado Puerta de Toledo
Stand 3134
☎ 91 364 18 76

Estación de Chamartín
Chamartin Railway Station
☎ 91 315 99 76

Barajas Airport
T-1 Terminal (international arrivals)
☎ 91 305 86 56

MONEY

The euro is the official currency of Spain, divided into 100 cents (or *centesimi*). Coins come in denominations of 1, 2, 5, 10, 20 and 50 cents, 1 and 2 euros, and bank notes come in denominations of 5, 10, 20, 50, 100, 200 and 500 euros (the last two are rarely seen). The notes and one side of the coins are the same throughout the European single currency zone, but each country has a different design on one face of each of the coins. Bank notes and coins from any of the other countries can be used in Spain.

TIPS/GRATUITIES

Yes ✓ No ✗		
Restaurants	✓	5–10%
Cafés/bars (if service not included)	✓	5%
Tour guides	✓	€1
Taxis	✓	5%
Chambermaids	✓	€1
Porters (per bag)	✓	€1
Toilet attendants	✗	no

BEING THERE

POSTAL SERVICES
The main post office, Palacio de Comunicaciones, on Plaza de la Cibeles, open Mon–Fri 8:30am–9:30pm, Sat 8:30–2, is being converted into the city hall. Elsewhere, *correos* (post offices) are open Mon–Sat 9–2. Stamps *(sellos)* are also sold in any *tabaco*, tobacconist shop identified by a brown and yellow sign. Post boxes are yellow.

TELEPHONES
There are plenty of telephone booths in the streets. Local calls are inexpensive. Although you can pay with coins, it is quicker and easier to buy a phonecard from any *tabaco* (tobacconist). Many phones also take credit cards. Long-distance calls are cheaper from a booth than from your hotel. Directory information is 003.

International dialling codes
From Madrid to:
UK: 00 44
Germany: 00 49
USA and Canada: 00 1
Netherlands: 00 31
France: 00 33

Emergency telephone numbers
Emergency: 112
Police: 091 (National), 092 (Madrid)
Fire: 080
Ambulance: 061
Red Cross: 91 522 22 22

EMBASSIES AND CONSULATES
UK: ☎ 91 308 52 01
USA: ☎ 91 587 22 00
Germany: ☎ 91 557 90 00
Netherlands: ☎ 91 353 75 00
France: ☎ 91 700 78 00

HEALTH ADVICE
Sun advice Madrid is at a high altitude and has a dry climate and strong sun, so use sunscreen, lip balm and skin moisturiser in spring and autumn as well as in high summer. Hats and sunglasses also give useful protection.

Drugs Prescription and non-prescription drugs are sold in *farmacias* (chemists), identified by a green cross. In central Madrid, the Farmacia Goya, Calle de Goya 89 ☎ 91 435 49 58 and the Farmacia Lastra, Calle del Conde de Peñalver 27 ☎ 91 402 43 01 are open 24 hours a day. If you are on medication, carry photocopies of the prescription.

PLANNING

Safe water Madrid is famous for the quality of its drinking water and, unlike many other Spanish cities, it does not have the taste of chlorine. Locals are always aware of the need to conserve water. In bathrooms, the hot tap is labelled 'c' for *caliente*, the cold has 'f' for *frío*.

PERSONAL SAFETY

As in most big cities, pickpockets are a problem in Madrid, especially in busy places such as open-air markets, large shops and railway stations. Valuables should be locked up in the hotel rather than carried with you. The Rastro Flea Market is a place where you need to be particularly careful. Madrid is a late-night city, but stay on main streets where there are more people. Be sure to take official taxis only (➤ 28).
City Police ☎ 092   Emergency ☎ 112

ELECTRICITY

The power supply in Madrid is 220 volts AC; sockets have two-pin plugs. If you have a British appliance, you will need an adaptor; North American appliances also require a transformer.

OPENING HOURS

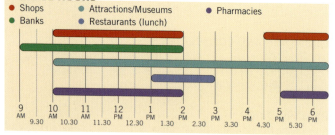

Major museums are open all day, but close on Monday or Tuesday. Smaller museums close for lunch. Shops vary, with most open Monday to Saturday. Some close Saturday afternoon, and most close all day Sunday. Department stores and malls are open 10–9. Many restaurants and shops close during August. During the San Isidro festival in May, banks close at noon. In July and August many offices work straight through from 8–3, then close. Apart from opening for Mass, well-known churches have set opening hours.

BEING THERE

LANGUAGE

The Spanish are pleased when foreigners try to speak their language. Don't worry about making mistakes; although they will correct them, it is always with a smile, and a sincere attempt to understand what you are trying to communicate. English is the most commonly taught foreign language; the younger generation usually knows a little and often quite a lot. Although pamphlets in foreign languages are available in the larger museums, signs and guided tours in foreign languages are rare.

hotel	*hotel*	one night	*una noche*
bed and breakfast	*pensión*	reservation	*reserva*
single room	*habitación individual*	chambermaid	*camarera*
double room	*habitación doble*	shower	*ducha*
one person	*una persona*	bath	*baño*
bank	*banco*	cheque	*cheque*
exchange office	*cambio*	traveller's cheque	*cheque de viaje*
post office	*correos*	credit card	*tarjeta de crédito*
coin	*moneda*	exchange rate	*cambio*
banknote	*billete*	commission	*comisión*
café	*cafetería*	dinner	*cena*
pub/bar	*bar*	table	*mesa*
breakfast	*desayuno*	waiter	*camarero*
lunch	*almuerzo*	waitress	*camarera*
airplane	*avión*	boat	*barca*
airport	*aeropuerto*	port	*puerta*
train	*tren*	ticket	*billete*
bus	*autobús*	single ticket	*billete de ida*
station	*estación*	bus stop	*parada*
yes	*sí*	hello	*hola*
no	*no*	goodbye	*adiós*
please/excuse me	*por favor*	good morning	*buenos días*
thank you	*gracias*	good afternoon	*buenas tardes*
you're welcome	*de nada*	goodnight	*buenas noches*

Best places to see

Monasterio de las Descalzas Reales	36–37
Museo de América	38–39
Museo Lázaro Galdiano	40–41
Museo Nacional Centro de Arte Reina Sofía	42–43
Museo del Prado	44–45
Museo Sorolla	46–47
Museo Thyssen-Bornemisza	48–49
Palacio Real	50–51
Parque del Retiro	52–53
Plaza Mayor	54–55

BEST PLACES TO SEE

1 Monasterio de las Descalzas Reales

www.patrimonionacional.es/
descreal/descreal.htm

Visit this 16th-century convent, still a closed order, not just to admire the notable art collection, but also to soak up the medieval atmosphere.

Behind the austere brick and stone façade, some 23 brown-robed nuns go about their quiet daily life.

BEST PLACES TO SEE

Opening hours are limited, so expect to queue. Groups are ushered in 20 at a time for a basic tour of the convent, which was founded in 1559 by Juana de Austria, daughter of Carlos V. The convent houses the Descalzas Reales (Barefoot Royal Sisters), women who initially came from the royal family and nobility (modern nuns are generally of humbler origin). As a dowry, each brought fine religious works of art by European masters such as Titian, Brueghel the Elder, van Eyck and Zurbarán.

The tour begins in the cloisters, then climbs the massive staircase past walls painted by Ximénez Donoso and Claudio Coello. The broad stone balustrade is carved from a single piece of granite. At the top, Felipe IV and the rest of the royal family look down from their painted balcony. All around the upper cloister are 16 elaborate chapels, the most important of which is dedicated to Virgen de Guadelupe. Don't miss the doll's house-like altar in one corner, designed to teach children about the sacred vessels used during Mass. In what was once the nuns' dormitory is the restored Salón de Tapices, hung with Flemish tapestries based on Rubens' cartoons (drawings). Peek out of the window at the kitchen garden, still tended by the sisters, even though they are overlooked by office buildings.

✚ 17J ✉ Plaza de las Descalzas Reales 3 ☎ 91 454 8800
🕐 Tue–Sat 10:30–12:45, 4–5:45, Sun, public hols 11–1:45. Closed Fri pm, all day Mon 💶 Inexpensive; free Wed to EU citizens 🚇 Callao, Sol, Opera 🚌 All routes to Puerta del Sol
❓ Visit by tour only, every 15 mins, duration 45 mins
ℹ Plaza Mayor 3 ☎ 91 588 16 36

BEST PLACES TO SEE

2 Museo de América

This museum's outstanding collection focuses on the art and culture of the Americas from before the Spanish colonial period to the present day.

If this museum were located on the Paseo del Prado, it would be packed with visitors. Set in the university district northwest of the city centre, it remains a well-kept secret. The spacious building has two floors of permanent exhibits, divided into five sections: Instruments of Knowledge, the American Reality, Society, Religion and Communication. Maps explain the movements of native peoples through the Americas and the routes of the explorers; feathered head-dresses contrast with ceramic vessels shaped like sting rays or parrots.

Since the Spanish melted down much of the gold they found in the Americas, the surviving Quimbayas treasure is particularly important. Dating from 600BC–AD600, the 130 gold objects were discovered in two tombs in Colombia. Finely crafted, they range from statuettes and bowls to necklaces and helmets. There is even a whistle and a trumpet.

Equally important are the codices, or manuscripts, which are keys to understanding pre-Colombian culture. One of only three surviving Mayan manuscripts is the *TroCortesiano Codex*, with symbols depicting the religious rituals of the Mayan calendar.

BEST PLACES TO SEE

Although the *Tudela Codex* also records religious ceremonies – this time of the late Aztec culture – it is post-conquest and dates from 1553. Written on paper and bound like a book, it is annotated in Spanish.

Paintings from the Spanish colonial period also serve as historical records, ranging from a large work showing the Archbishop and Viceroy Morcillo entering the city of Potosí (modern Bolivia) to a series of portraits of the multiracial society of Mexico.

🚇 3B ✉ Avenida de los Reyes Católicos 6 ☎ 91 543 94 37/91 549 26 41
🕐 Tue–Sat 9:30–3; Sun, public hols 10–3
✋ Inexpensive; free under-18, over-65; Sun 🍴 Café (€)
🚇 Moncloa, Islas Filipinas
🚌 1, 12, 16, 44, 46, 61, 82, 113, 132, 133 ❓ Foreign-language audioguides
ℹ Plaza Mayor 3
☎ 91 588 16 36

3 Museo Lázaro Galdiano

www.flg.es

The former home of publisher and collector José Lázaro Galdiano (1862–1947) contains dazzling paintings and priceless objets d'art.

The neo-Renaissance *palazzo*, the Parque Florido, north of the city centre, dates from 1903. The exhibition begins on the ground floor with an assessment of Galdiano's intentions and achievments and offers a taster of what lies in store. Rare books and manuscripts, exquisite caskets of enameled wood, gold and silverware, rock crystal and gemstones, medieval stained glass and Renaissance bronzes all vie for attention. Look for El Greco's magnificent *Adoration of the Magi* (room 2) and the 15th-century sword presented to Pope Innocent VIII by the Count of Tendilla (room 3).

Spanish paintings and scultpure are on the first floor in the former private apartments. Apart from the triptychs and panel paintings by medieval masters like Bartolome de Castro, there are canvases by El Greco, Murillo, Zurbarán, José de Ribera, Velázquez and Luís Paret. Don't miss Goya's spooky *Witches Sabath (Cabinete)* and in the adjoining room (13) the Godoy table, fashioned from mahogany, marble and gilded bronze in 1800. The second floor is devoted to European Art from the 15th to the 19th centuries. Most of the major schools are represented and there are works by Quentin Metsys, Hieronymous Bosch, Brueghel the

Younger, Cranach, Dürer, Rembrandt, van Dyck and Tiepolo among the displays of Limoges enamels, Sèvres porcelain, cut glass, ivories, French table clocks and miniatures. Admirers of Constable, Gainsborough, Lawrence and Sir Joshua Reynolds are in for a treat.

🕂 11C ✉ Calle de Serrano 122 ☎ 91 561 60 84
🕐 Wed–Mon 10–4:30 ✋ Inexpensive; free under-12; Sun free for all EU citizens 🚇 Rubén Darío, Núñez del Balboa, Gregorio Marañon 🚌 12, 16, 51, 61 ❓ Free guided tour Sat, Sun 11:30am
ℹ Calle del Duque de Medinaceli 2 ☎ 91 429 49 51

4 Museo Nacional Centro de Arte Reina Sofía

www.museoreinasofia.es

One of the largest buildings in Europe houses Spain's national museum of modern art, including the world-famous painting, *Guernica* by Picasso.

The two glass elevators slide up and down the outside of what was an 18th-century hospital. Two floors are devoted to the permanent collection of paintings and sculptures from the late 19th century to the present day; temporary exhibitions are held in the dramatic annexe, opened in 2005.

Start up on the fourth floor. Room 26 is dominated by the gigantic canvases of Robert Motherwell

BEST PLACES TO SEE

(USA) and Antoni Tàpies (Spain; also Rooms 27, 28). Pablo Palazuelo's geometric patterns make your eyes ache (Room 25), while his fellow-*madrileño*, Eduardo Arroyo (Room 31), prefers a big, bright palette. A star of the contemporary sculpture scene is Eduardo Chillida, whose massive metal works fill Rooms 34 and 35.

The biggest crowds are on the second floor. As you approach Room 6, you can hear the hum of conversation in the rooms dedicated to Picasso.

The main focus is *Guernica* (1937), Picasso's powerful work condemning the unjustifiable bombing of the Basque town of Guernica during the Spanish Civil War. Picasso's will stated that the painting could only be brought to Spain when democracy was restored. In 1981, six years after Franco's death, *Guernica* was finally shown in Spain.

It is not the only politically inspired painting on display here. Rooms 10 and 11 are devoted to Dalí, whose *Enigma of Hitler* (1939) also reflects the uncertainty of those times. Nearby rooms feature works by Joan Miró, Juan Gris and surrealist painters Max Ernst and René Magritte.

🚇 19L ✉ Calle Santa Isabel 52 ☎ 91 467 50 62 🕐 Mon, Wed–Sat 10–9, Sun 10–2:30 💰 Moderate; free under-18, over-65; Sat 2:30–9, Sun 🍴 Restaurant/café (€) 🚇 Atocha 🚌 All routes to Atocha ❓ The *Abono Paseo del Arte/BonoArte* ticket is a reduced rate, combined ticket (➤ 16)

BEST PLACES TO SEE

5 Museo del Prado

www.museoprado.es

The ongoing expansion of Museo del Prado, one of the world's great museums, will enable it to display more of its superb collections of art.

The 18th-century Edificio Villanueva on the Paseo del Prado will continue to house masterpieces by Bosch, Goya, El Greco, Murillo, Rubens, Titian, Velázquez and Zurbarán. Temporary exhibitions will be shown in the dramatic annexe, opened in 2007; the renovation of the Casón del Buen Retiro continues. It helps if you rent one of the audio-guides and focus on a favourite artist or era.

Not surprisingly, the range of Spanish art from the 11th to the 19th century is unparalleled, especially from the *Siglo de Oro*, the golden 17th century. Foremost was Velázquez (1599–1660), court painter to Felipe IV. His works, such as *Las Meninas* (The Maids of Honour) and *Las Hilanderas* (The Spinners) are turning points in the art of composition. A century later, Goya (1746–1828) was, arguably, even more influential. His range was extraordinary, from his naked *Maja* (Courtesan) to the *Fusilamientos del 3 de mayo*. This patriotic, passionate painting commemorates the heroism of the *madrileño* revolt against the French invaders in May 1808. Most disturbing of all are his 14 *Pinturas Negras* (Black Paintings) from the end of his life. *Saturn devouring one of his sons* and *Witches' Sabbath* make anything but comfortable viewing.

Don't miss *The Garden of Delights* by the Flemish master Hieronymus Bosch (1450–1516).

BEST PLACES TO SEE

Despite years of academic study, this allegorical triptych portraying human frailties has yet to be fully deciphered.

✚ 20K ✉ Paseo del Prado s/n ☎ 91 330 28 00, 24-hour phone; 906 322 222 🕐 Tue–Sun 9–7, public hols 9–2. Closed Mon, 1 Jan, Good Friday, 1 May, 25 Dec
✋ Moderate; free under-18s, over-65s; Sun 9–7
🍴 Restaurant/café (€) Ⓜ Atocha, Banco de España 🚌 9, 10, 14, 19, 27, 34, 37, 45
❓ *Abono Paseo del Arte/BonoArte* ticket: reduced rate for Prado, Museo Thyssen-Bornemisza and Museo Nacional Centro de Arte Reina Sofía. For the latest changes at the Prado, check their website
ℹ Calle del Duque de Medinaceli 2 ☎ 902 100 007

BEST PLACES TO SEE

6 Museo Sorolla

http://museosorolla.mcu.es

A well-furnished mansion, a fine art gallery and a painter's studio all in one, the home of Joaquín Sorolla (1863–1923) is a gem.

With its Moorish gardens and trickling fountains, the atmosphere at the Museo Sorolla, built in 1911, is in total contrast to the formality and grandeur of Madrid's major museums. Born in Valencia, Sorolla worked in Paris and Rome before becoming the darling of European and American high society.

BEST PLACES TO SEE

Often labelled 'the Spanish Impressionist', Sorolla had no connection with that movement. Passionate about Spain and the Spanish, his treatment of sharp light and heavy shade was both individual and highly accomplished. While he lived in Madrid (1910–23), his large paintings, with their bold and lively brushwork of people in sun-dappled landscapes, were in great demand.

In the first room you see the romantic side of Sorolla. Don't miss *Madre* (1895), a simple scene of a tired mother and her newborn. Walk through the second room with its jolly beach scenes to Sorolla's studio. Here the soaring walls are covered in canvases, including several of his wife, Clotilde.

Sorolla's finest work is upstairs. His studies for a series for the Hispanic Society of New York include rustic types in colourful regional costume, a bagpiper and a Don Quixote lookalike from La Mancha, complete with donkey and windmills and a large painting of four women taking a siesta. In galleries on the ground floor (enter from the garden) is Sorolla's fine collection of antique Spanish pottery, as well as some lively sketches of Central Park, New York.

✚ 10C ✉ Paseo del General Martínez Campos 37 ☎ 91 310 15 84 🕒 Tue, Thu–Sat 9:30–3, Wed 9:30–6, Sun, public hols 10–3 💶 Inexpensive; free for under-18s, over-65s and Sun 🍴 Plenty near by (€) Ⓜ Iglesia, Rubén Darío, Gregorio Marañon 🚌 5, 7, 16, 40, 61, 147
ℹ Calle del Duque de Medinaceli 2 ☎ 902 100 007

47

7 Museo Thyssen-Bornemisza

www.museothyssen.org

The Thyssen-Bornemisza family built the world's finest art collection. It moved to Madrid in 1992, completing the city's golden triangle of museums.

The spacious 19th-century Palacio de Villahermosa is the perfect setting for an art history lesson spanning seven centuries of European and American art. The lesson begins on the top floor, where the 13th- to 15th-century religious works positively glow, thanks to excellent lighting. Next come a succession of fascinating early Renaissance portraits. In Room 5, near Hans Holbein the Younger's classic portrait of Henry VIII of England, is Francesco Cossa's intriguing 15th-century *Portrait of a Man*. This is an experiment in *trompe l'oeil* and perspective as a hand holds out a ring for you to inspect. Room 20 has two Flemish masterpieces, lit as fiercely as a movie set: *Esau selling his Birthright* (1627) by Hendrik ter Brugghen and *Supper at Emmaus* (1633) by Matthias Stom.

The tour continues past Titian and Caravaggio, Impressionists and Expressionists. On the ground floor are eight rooms of 20th-century works. In Room 41, works by Picasso and Braque represent Cubism. Room 45 is lined with 20th-century works: Picasso's

BEST PLACES TO SEE

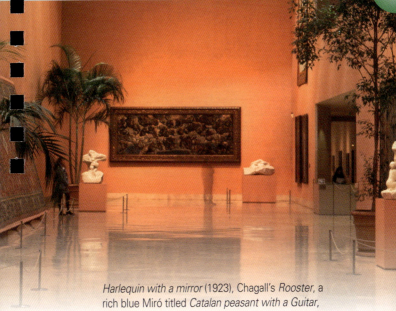

Harlequin with a mirror (1923), Chagall's *Rooster*, a rich blue Miró titled *Catalan peasant with a Guitar*, plus others by Braque, Léger, Kandinsky, Ernst and Juan Gris. Room 47 focuses on star American names such as Edward Hopper, whose *Hotel Room* (1931) has a typically lonely and mysterious atmosphere. A glass pavilion houses 19th- and 20th-century paintings from Baroness Carmen Thyssen-Bornemisza's collection.

✚ 19J ✉ Paseo del Prado 8 ☎ 91 369 01 51 🕐 Tue–Sun 10–7. Closed 1 Jan, 1 May, 25 Dec ✋ Moderate, reduction for over 65s and students; free for children under 12
🍴 Restaurant/café (€) Ⓜ Banco de España 🚌 1, 2, 5, 9, 10, 14, 15, 20, 27, 34, 37, 45, 51, 52, 53, 74, 146, 150
❓ Less crowded Wed–Fri lunchtime. Temporary exhibitions, El Mirador del Musei restaurant open until 11pm Jul, Aug. *The Abono Paseo del Arte/BonoArte* ticket is a reduced rate ticket for the Prado, Museo Thyssen-Bornemisza and Museo Nacional Centro de Arte Reina Sofía

BEST PLACES TO SEE

8 Palacio Real

www.patrimonionacional.es

With a grand parade ground, fabulous views over the city, imposing staircases and ornate rooms, this is everything that a royal palace should be.

All that is missing is the royal family, who prefer to live in the Zarzuela Palace on the outskirts of Madrid. Today, the grand 250-year-old Palacio Real is used solely for state occasions. To get the most out of your visit, join a 45-minute tour, then wander

BEST PLACES TO SEE

round at your leisure. As you climb the main staircase, imagine the red carpet treatment and guard of honour that greets new ambassadors and visiting heads of state. Each room seems more magnificent than the last. With its backdrop of 17th-century Flemish tapestries, the Sala de Columnas is often used for ceremonies. Curiously, no one sits on the two thrones in the Throne Room because King Juan Carlos and Queen Sofía prefer to stand during audiences. Continue past great paintings by Goya and admire ornate clocks, then prepare yourself for Gasparini's Robing Room. This jewel box of a room, with a marble floor and decorated walls and ceiling, is now used for taking coffee after state banquets.

The banqueting hall has a grand ceiling fresco of Christopher Columbus offering the world to the *Reyes Católicos*, Fernando and Isabel. Outside the palace, the Real Armería (Royal Armoury) has undergone a facelift, installing the latest museum technology for its world-class collection. Temporary exhibitions are also held; most are free, with direct access from the street.

The entry ticket includes the Royal Pharmacy and the impressive Royal Armoury, with weapons dating back to the 13th century.

✛ 15J ✉ Calle Bailén s/n ☎ 91 454 88 00 ◷ Summer: Mon–Sat 9–6, Sun, public hols 9–3. Winter: Mon–Sat 9:30–5, Sun, public hols 9–2. Closed on official occasions ✋ Moderate 🍴 Cafeteria (€) Ⓜ Opera 🚌 3, 25, 39, 148 ❓ Multilingual guided tours. Changing of the Guard at 12, 1st Wed of month Jan–Jun, Oct–Dec. Telephone to confirm ℹ Plaza Mayor 27 ☎ 91 588 16 36

BEST PLACES TO SEE

Parque del Retiro

The 120ha (295-acre) park, with its mixture of formal gardens, tree-studded lawns and a large lake, acts as a set of lungs to refresh the city centre.

Felipe IV created this Buen Retiro (a pleasant place to retire or retreat) in the 17th century. This is where the court came to have fun, staying in the Buen Retiro Palace and watching bullfights, plays and fireworks in the gardens. A century later, Carlos III opened the royal park to the public – as long as they were dressed properly. By the mid-19th century, anyone could enjoy the park, whatever their garb.

Nowadays, a Sunday stroll is a must. *Madrileños* promenade along the Paseo del Estanque, while children play and watch noisy puppet shows. Take in a free band concert (from May–Oct) at the Templete de la Musica, have your portrait sketched or try your luck at the roulette wheels of the *chulapos*, colourful locals in waistcoats and caps. There are pathways for cyclists and rollerbladers, shady spots for picnicking and formal parterres with botanical name-plates to identify the species.

Important landmarks include the elaborate 1922 memorial and statue of Alfonso XII, *El Pacificador*

BEST PLACES TO SEE

(the Peacemaker), which overlooks the *estanque* (lake). Check whether there are any exhibitions in the two glass halls, the Palacio de Cristal and Palacio de Velázquez, both built in the 1880s, or a *zarzuela* concert in the Casa de Vacas (House of Cows), which is on the site of an old dairy. La Rosaleda (Rose Garden) is at its best in May. Avoid the park after dark.

✚ 22K ✉ Calle de Alfonso XII 🕓 May–Sep 6am–midnight; Oct–Apr 6am–10pm ✋ Free 🚇 Atocha, Ibiza, Retiro 🚌 1, 2, 15, 19, 20, 26, 28, 51, 52, 61, 68, 74, 146
ℹ Calle del Duque de Medinaceli 2 ☎ 902 100 007

BEST PLACES TO SEE

10 Plaza Mayor

Traffic-free and large enough to swallow a crowd of 50,000, one of the most handsome squares in Europe is dominated by a royal statue.

The bronze equestrian statue of Felipe III makes a popular meeting point. The reliefs around the four giant lampposts spell out the history of the plaza. In 1617, under Felipe III, the old square was replaced by this new arena, created to hold everything from bullfights to theatre, festivals to inquisitions. Its inauguration coincided with the beatification of San Isidro, Madrid's patron saint, in 1620.

Throughout the year, tourists and locals alike watch the world go by from café tables that spill across the paving stones. During the annual San Isidro festivities in May, giant *cocidos* (stews) and *paellas* are served up, and in summer there are concerts and plays. The annual Christmas market, with its traditional sweets, cakes and toys, has been a feature since 1837. The Casa de la Panadería, the dominant building on the north side, dates from 1590, but the murals were only added in 1992. The oldest shop on the square is Bustillo (No 4), where they have been selling cloth since 1790.

Since 1927, the arcades have been filled with tables for the popular stamp and coin collectors' market on Sunday mornings. In fact, anything that can be collected is displayed and offered for sale: postcards, cheese labels, pins and lottery tickets.

✚ 16J ✉ Plaza Mayor 💰 Free 🍴 Botín (➤ 84–85)
🚇 Sol, La Latina, Opéra 🚌 3, 5, 15, 17, 18, 20, 23, 31, 35, 50, 51, 52, 53, 65, 150
ℹ Plaza Mayor 27 ☎ 91 588 16 36

BEST PLACES TO SEE

Best things to do

Good places to have lunch	58–59
Great views	60–61
Best galleries	62–63
Great cafés and bars	64–65
Best souvenir buys	66–67
Best *tapas* bars	68–69
Places to take the children	70–71
Sporting activities	72–73
A walk along Calle de Alcalá	74–75
Peace and quiet	76–77

BEST THINGS TO DO

Good places to have lunch

Angel (€)
Near the Gran Vía but away from the tourists, this tiny, atmospheric bistro is ideal for an intimate lunch.
✉ Augusto Figueroa 35 ☎ 91 521 70 12

Brasserie de Lista (€)
In Madrid's poshest shopping district. This stylish yet informal restaurant serves international dishes, with grilled meat a speciality. Sit outside under the parasols and count the carrier bags with designer labels passing by.
✉ Serrano 10 ☎ 91 411 08 67

Casa Labra (€)
Eat cod at the birthplace of the Spanish Socialist Party. The speciality is *soldaditos de Pavía*, mouthfuls of deep-fried cod. Off Puerta del Sol.
✉ Calle de Tuetuán 12 ☎ 91 513 00 81

BEST THINGS TO DO

Casa Mingo (€)
After seeing the Goya ceiling next door, everyone comes here for roast chicken, sausages and cider – plain, simple and cheap.
✉ Glorieta de San Antonio de la Florida 34 ☎ 91 547 79 18

A' Casiña (€€€)
Located in the Casa de Campo, so lunching here is like eating out in the country. Try the Galician specialities, especially the seafood.
✉ Avenida del Angel s/n ☎ 91 526 34 25

El Espejo (€)
Here you can linger over a coffee or beer and *tapas* on the outdoor terrace of this pavilion overlooking Paseo de Recoletos (➤ 120).
✉ Paseo de Recoletos 31 ☎ 91 308 23 47

Gran Café Gijón (€)
Order the menu of the day for a bargain lunch in plush art nouveau surroundings.
✉ Paseo de Recoletos 21 ☎ 91 521 54 25

Hotel Ritz (€€–€€€)
The shady garden, scented by flowers, is a delightful spot for Sunday brunch. Expensive but worth it.
✉ Plaza de la Lealtad 5 ☎ 91 701 67 67

Museo Thyssen-Bornemisza (€)
Have a coffee at the counter or take a table to order one of the modern Spanish dishes. You can sit outside in fine weather.
✉ Paseo del Prado 8 ☎ 91 369 01 51

La Posada de la Villa (€€–€€€)
Stop in this medieval tavern for a taste of some traditional, hearty dishes. Famous for its roasted, milk-fed lamb.
✉ Calle de la Cava Baja 9 ☎ 91 366 18 60

Great views

From the glass elevators on the outside of the Museo Nacional Centro de Arte Reina Sofía (➤ 42–43).

From the top of Faro de Madrid, Avenida de los Reyes Católicos (☎ 91 544 81 04; currently closed for repairs).

From the swimming pool at the top of the Hotel Emperador, Gran Vía 53 (☎ 91 547 28 00).

From a cable-car on the Teleférico (➤ 148).

From a café in the Jardines de las Vistillas.

From the terrace restaurant on top of the Thyssen-Bornemisza Museum; only on summer nights (➤ 48–49).

From the roof terrace of the Teatro Real in summer (➤ 112).

From the new Realcafé Bernabéu, a themed café looking down into the Real Madrid football stadium (➤ 134).

From the Penthouse bar of the ME Madrid Reina Victoria Hotel on the Plaza Santa Ana.

From the Campo del Moro, for a great view of the Palacio Real (➤ 50–51).

BEST THINGS TO DO

BEST THINGS TO DO

Best galleries

Major companies have invested in modern art collections that are open to the public during office hours:

Fundación La Caixa, Calle Serrano 60 (☎ 91 426 0202)

Fundación Carlos de Amberes, Calle Clandio Coello 99 (☎ 91 435 22 01)

Fundación Juan March, Calle de Castelló 77 (☎ 91 435 42 40)

Fundación Mapfre Vida, Avenida General Perón 40 (☎ 91 581 16 28)

Fundación Telefónica, Fuencarral 3 (➤ 148; ☎ 91 584 2300)

Museo Picasso – Coleccíon Arias, Plaza de Picasso 1 (☎ 91 868 00 56)

Palacio de Cristal, Parque del Retiro (➤ 53; ☎ 91 574 66 14)

Sala de Exposiciones de Alcalá, Calle de Alcalá 31 (☎ 91 720 81 17)

Sala de Exposiciones – Canal de Isabel II, Calle Santa Engracia 125 (☎ 91 720 81 23)

Sala de Exposiciones del Círculo de Bellas Artes, Calle de Alcalá 42 (☎ 91 360 54 00)

BEST THINGS TO DO

Great cafés and bars

El Balcón de Rosales (€)
On the pretty *paseo* overlooking the Casa de Campo, this disco-bar is popular with the younger set who come here for Tex-Mex food.
✉ Paseo del Pintor Rosales ☎ 91 541 74 40 🕒 8pm–dawn. Closed Sun–Thu 🚇 Argüelles

Café del Foro (€)
Tiny bar with arresting tiled décor. Serves canapés, but if you're really hungry there's a restaurant at the back.
✉ Calle San Andrés 38 ☎ 91 445 37 52 🕒 9am–2am. Closed Sun 🚇 Bilbao

Café Isadora (€)
The décor pays tribute to American dancer Isadora Duncan. Snacks available as well as cocktails and unusual liqueur coffees.
✉ Calle Divino Pastor 14 ☎ 91 445 71 54 🕒 4pm–2am 🚇 Bilbao

Café Manuela (€)
Popular student haunt. Serves cocktails snacks and draught beer.
✉ Calle San Vicente Ferrer 29 ☎ 91 531 70 37 🕒 6pm–3am (Fri, Sat 4pm–3am) 🚇 Tribunal, Noviciado

Cervecería Alemana (€)
Yet another watering-hole where Hemingway once drank, this 1904 German-style beer house even uses steins. Wood panelling and white marble-topped tables add to the atmosphere.
✉ Plaza de Santa Ana 6 ☎ 91 429 70 33 🕒 10:30am–12:30am (Fri, Sat to 2am). Closed Tue 🚇 Antón Martín, Sevilla, Sol

Chocolatería San Ginés (€)
All green tiles and mirrors, this small café is a favourite for hot chocolate and *churros*. At 3:30am it is packed with partygoers from the nightclub next door.
✉ Pasadizo de San Ginés 5 ☎ 91 365 65 46 🕒 9:30am–7am 🚇 Sol

Embassy (€)
Founded in 1931, this sophisticated boulevard café-tea room has its own *pâtisserie*, specializing in mouth-watering, French-style cakes. It also serves cocktails and elegant snacks.
✉ Paseo de la Castellana 12 (also branches at Ayala 3 and La Moraleja) ☎ 91 435 94 80 🕓 9am–midnight Ⓜ Colón, Serrano

Parnasillo (€)
A busy cocktail and snack bar in the heart of the atmospheric Malasaña district with décor from the belle époque period.
✉ Calle San Andrés 33 ☎ 91 447 00 79 🕓 2:30pm–3am Ⓜ Bilbao

Populart (€)
Late-night live music is the speciality at this 'Café Jazz'. Expect to pay a small cover charge to listen to jazz, plus anything from flamenco to reggae.
✉ Calle de las Huertas 22 ☎ 91 429 84 07 🕓 4pm–2:30am (Fri, Sat to 4:30am) Ⓜ Antón Martín

La Venencia (€)
If a chair is propping the door ajar, this 1929 bar is open for business. Sample sherries, from the sweetest to the driest. Simple *tapas*, *mojama* (salty dried tuna) and olives.
✉ Calle de Echegaray 7 ☎ 91 429 73 13 🕓 1–3:30pm, 7:30pm–2am. Closed Aug Ⓜ Sevilla, Sol

BEST THINGS TO DO

Best souvenir buys

A fan, an accessory that is still in use, especially in the heat of summer; or as a fashion statement. From Casa de Diego (Plaza de la Puerta del Sol 12 ☎ 91 522 66 43).

A Real Madrid football shirt from the Bernabéu Stadium shop.

A CD of guitar music, such as blind composer Joaquín Rodrigo's popular *Concierto de Aranjuez*, inspired by the cool, peaceful gardens in the grounds of the Palacio Real in Aranjuez.

A *puchero,* a glazed clay pot from the Rastro flea market, used for food or even for flowers.

A genuine hand-made guitar from a craftsman such as Javier Rojo Solar, established for over 50 years (Divino Pastor 22 ☎ 91 445 72 19).

A pair of hand-stitched *alpargatas,* rope-soled sandals from Maxi Garbayo at the Antigua Casa Crespo, founded in 1863 (Divino Pastor 29 ☎ 91 521 56 54).

Anything leather, from shoes to handbags, from any branch of the El Corte Inglés department store.

A hand-painted ceramic vase or plate from a specialist shop such as the 100-year-old Antigua Casa Talavera (Isabel la Católica 2 ☎ 91 547 34 17).

Sugared violets, tiny sweets made with real violets, from La Violeta (Plaza de Canalejas 6 ☎ 91 522 55 22).

A handsome black cape with a scarlet silk lining from Capas Seseña, another 100-year-old Madrid store (Calle Cruz 23 ☎ 91 531 68 40).

Best *tapas* bars

Alkalde (€–€€€)
A *tapas* bar with a difference: the Basque name is a clue to the Basque-style *tapas*, which include *tortilla* with red peppers and seafood.
✉ Calle de Jorge Juan 10 ☎ 91 576 33 59 🕐 Lunch, dinner 🚇 Serrrano, Retiro

El Almendro 13 (€)
This bar specializes in hearty Andalucian cooking, so ask for a *manzanilla* from Sanlúcar with your *tapas*. If you order a *ración* (large portion), a bell is rung when it is ready.
✉ Calle del Almendro 13 ☎ 91 365 42 52 🕐 Lunch, dinner 🚇 La Latina

El Anciano Rey de los Vinos (€)
Founded in 1909, this bar near the Palacio Real is atmospheric, with mirrors and tiles. Try sugary, crunchy *torrijas*, the surprising speciality that is a perfect partner for their own sweet muscatel wines.
✉ Calle de Bailén 19 ☎ 91 559 53 32 🕐 Lunch, dinner. Closed Wed, Sun, Aug 🚇 La Latina

Antigua Casa Angel Sierra (€)
This 1917, old Madrid-style vermouth bar has painted glass and rows of bottles. Vermouth with *(con sifón)* or without soda, is served from a massive brass tap, as is beer. Simple *tapas* are made in front of you.

✉ Calle de la Gravina 11 ☎ 91 531 01 26 🕐 Lunch, dinner (no credit cards) 🚇 Chueca

BEST THINGS TO DO

La Ardosa (€)
Copies of Goya prints line the walls of this atmospheric *taberna*. Czech beers are a big draw, as are the *tapas* and *raciones*.
✉ Calle Colón 13 ☎ 91 521 49 79 🕔 11:30am–1:30am 🚇 Tribunal

Casa del Abuelo (€)
Handy for Plaza Santa Ana, 'Grandad's place' dates from 1906 and has retained its no-nonsense, spit and sawdust atmosphere. Wine is usually preferred with shrimp, the house speciality.
✉ Calle Victoria 12 ☎ 91 521 2319 🕔 11:30–3:30, 6:30–11:30 🚇 Sol

Casa Alberto (€€)
Legend has it that Cervantes came here while writing *Don Quixote*. Order a *Vermut de Grifo* (draught vermouth drawn from a splendid antique pump) and try the *albôndigas* (meatballs).
✉ Calle de Las Huertas 18 ☎ 91 429 93 56 🕔 Lunch, dinner. Closed Sun dinner, Mon 🚇 Sol, Tirso de Molina

La Dolores (€)
This traditional *taberna* has preserved its original 1908 tiled façade. Always busy on account of its famous canapés (ask for *pulgas*).
✉ Plaza de Jesús 4 ☎ 91 429 22 43 🕔 11am–1am 🚇 Antón Martín

Los Gatos (€)
Bags of atmosphere in this locals' haunt, famous for its décor. Arrive before 2pm if you want a seat for lunch (mainly *tapas*).
✉ Calle Jesús 2 ☎ 91 429 30 67 🕔 Lunch, dinner (no credit cards). Closed Sun 🚇 Antón Martín

Las Letras (€–€€)
This bar specializes in up-market *tapas* – *menu del dia* also available. Additional seating upstairs.
✉ Calle Echegaray 26 ☎ 91 429 48 43 🕔 Noon–1am. Closed Sun, Mon 🚇 Sol, Antón Martín

BEST THINGS TO DO

Places to take the children

Aquasur
This park is 540km (25 miles) south of the city, near Aranjuez. The most daring water slide is the Spirotubo, a steep, scary tube ride, but there are also gentler water slides, a zoo, mini-golf and a swimming pool.
✉ Carretera de Andalucía (N-IV) km 44 ☎ 91 891 60 34
🕐 Jun–Sep 11–8, 11 at weekends 💰 Expensive

Aquópolis San Fernando de Henares
At San Fernando de Henares, 15km (9 miles) east of Madrid, this is a huge lake in a wooded park. Rides range from easy (Foam) to the most scary (Kamikaze), an 85m-long (280ft) slide with a 40m (130ft) drop.
✉ Carretera Nacional II, 15.5km ☎ 91 673 10 13; www.aquapolis.es 🕐 Jun, Sep 12–7; Jul, Aug 12–8 💰 Expensive

Aquópolis Villa Nueva de la Cañada
Attractions here include the 40m-high (130ft) Kamikaze and the Tobogán Blando, with a series of harmless jumps and turns. Upgraded in 1999, the park has more trees and prettier gardens. It's located about 40km (25 miles) northwest of Madrid via M 503, exit 8.
✉ Avenida de la Dehesa, Villanueva de la Cañada ☎ 91 815 69 33; www.aquapolis.es 🕐 Jun, Sep 12–7; Jul, Aug 12–8 💰 Expensive

Faunia
The only theme park in Europe devoted to nature and biodiversity. Eight pavilions re-create different ecosystems (jungle, polar region etc), with authentic sights, sounds, smells, flora and fauna, including 3,500 animals and 1,000 plant species. Experience a tropical storm first hand!
✉ Avenida de las Comunidades 28 ☎ 91 301 62 35; www.faunia.es 🕐 Daily from 10am; hours vary according to season and day of week. Check 💰 Expensive 🚇 Valdebernardo

BEST THINGS TO DO

Parque de Atracciones
This permanent funfair in Casa de Campo (➤ 76–77) has about 40 rides as well as the usual amusements. One of the most popular thrill rides is the Virtual Simulator.
✉ Casa de Campo ☎ 91 463 29 00; www.parquedeatracciones.es
🕒 Daily 12–7; later in summer. Closed weekdays Sep–Apr
💰 Expensive 🚇 Batán

Safari de Madrid
Some 50km (30 miles) west of the city, this is a traditional safari park with elephants, lions and tigers. There are also reptile and snake houses and, in July and August, go-karts, mini-motorbikes and a swimming pool.
✉ Aldea de Fresno, Carretera de Extremadura, N-V, 32km ☎ 91 862 23 14; www.safarimadrid.com 🕒 Daily from 10:30. Closes 8 summer, 7 autumn, 5:30 winter, 6:30 spring 💰 Expensive

Tren de la Fresa
Take the 'Strawberry Train' down to Aranjuez (➤ 160). The old steam train departs from Atocha Railway Station. Once in the town, there is plenty of time to enjoy the gardens, riverboat rides and the royal palace
☎ 902 240 202 🕒 Apr–Jun weekends and public hols. Leaves Atocha 10am, returning 6:30pm 💰 Expensive

Warnerbros Park
This theme park on the outskirts of Madrid has five areas: Hollywood Boulevard, Cartoon Village, the Wild West Territory, Super Heroes and Warner Brothers Studios. No food or drink may be brought into the park.
✉ San Martin de la Vega. NIV to km22, then M-506 and follow signs ☎ 91 821 12 34; www.warnerbrospark.com 🕒 Summer daily 11–11; spring, autumn weekends, hols 11–8; winter weekends, hols 12–7. Times vary, check 💰 Expensive 🚆 C3 from Atocha

71

BEST THINGS TO DO

Sporting activities

SPECTATOR SPORTS
Basketball
Real Madrid's basketball team has a record that was, until recently, almost as dazzling as the football squad. Real plays in the Palacio Raimundo Saporta from Sep to May.

✉ Paseo de la Castellana 259 ☎ 91 315 00 46 🕒 Box office: 11–2, 5–8 🚇 Goya

Football
Atlético Madrid, perennial rivals of Real Madrid (➤ 134 for details), play in a 60,000-seat stadium. Since returning to the first division in 2002, they have been attempting to recapture the form of 1996 when they won the league and cup.

✉ Estadio Vicente Calderón, Paseo Virgen del Puerto 67 ☎ 91 366 47 07 🕒 Box office: 5–8. Closed Sat, Sun 🚇 Pirámides

PARTICIPATORY SPORTS
Golf
With the success of Seve Ballesteros and José María Olazábal, golf is enjoying a boom in Spain. Although it can be expensive, there is a good choice of 18-hole golf courses around Madrid.

Club de Campo Villa de Madrid

✉ Carretera de Castilla, 2km ☎ 91 550 20 10; www.clubvillademadrid.com 🚌 160, 161

Ice-skating
Dreams Palacio de Hielo
There is more to do than ice-skate in this 'Palace of Ice'. Opened in 2003, this multi-purpose leisure and shopping complex is halfway between downtown Madrid and Barajas Airport. There are some 20 places to eat, 15 cinema screens, 24 bowling lanes and, of course, ice skating. Open from morning until late evening, but phone to see what is on, and when.

✉ Calle Silvano 77, Canillas ☎ 91 716 01 59 (ice-skating); 91 716 00 45

BEST THINGS TO DO

(bowling) 🕐 Hours vary, check listings magazines 🚇 Canillas 🚌 73, 112, 120, 122

Skiing
On weekends skiers head for the mountains north of the city, an hour or so away by car. Resorts include:
Navacerrada ☎ 91 852 1435; La Pinilla ☎ 92 155 03 04; Valcotos ☎ 91 563 30 61

Xanadu
The large indoor ski slope is the centrepiece of this vast new shopping and entertainment complex. Slopes for novices and professionals, a ski school and equipment rental.
✉ Carratera NV km 23 Arroyomolinos ☎ 902 263 026 🕐 Mon–Thu, Sun public hols 10am–midnight 🚌 528 from Príncipe Pio

Swimming
There are indoor and open-air pools run by the city. In the Casa de Campo there is one for children, one intermediate and one of Olympic size. All are busy on summer weekends. See also Aquasur and Aquópolis (➤ 70).
✉ Casa de Campo, Avenida del Angel ☎ 91 463 00 50 🕐 Indoor: 9:45–8. Outdoor: (summer only) 11–9 🚇 Lago

BEST THINGS TO DO

a walk along Calle de Alcalá

Start at the Banco de España Metro station and walk west.

The Calle de Alcalá runs east towards the university town of Alcalá de Henares. On the north side, where it converges with the Gran Vía, is the 19th-century Iglesia de San José, popular with South Americans who want to see where early 19th-century revolutionary hero, Simón Bolívar was married. Opposite is the elaborate 1926 Círculo de Bellas Artes (No 42), an arts club with a café and outdoor terrace. Anyone can pay a small fee to see current exhibitions and eat in the Cafetería La Pecera.

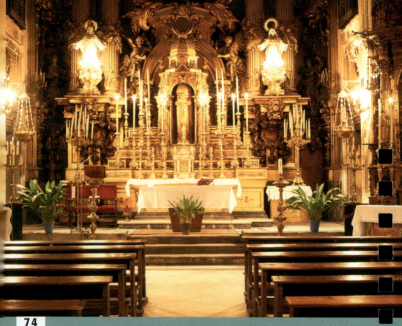

BEST THINGS TO DO

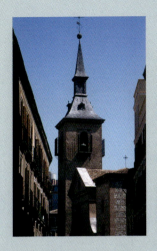

Cross over and continue on the north side of the Calle de Alcalá.

At No 25 is the Iglesia de las Calatravas (➤ 88–89), a church with an ornate façade. A few doors down is the Casino de Madrid (No 15), a private gentleman's club, not a gambling casino. No 13 is the Museo de la Real Academia de Bellas Artes de San Fernando (➤ 94–95) and No 3 is the massive Ministry of Finance, which was built as the Customs House in the 18th century. The next square is the busy Puerta del Sol (➤ 100–101).

Continue across the square to the Calle del Arenal with its busy shops and restaurants.

The first church on the left is San Ginés, with a painting by El Greco in an adjacent chapel. The walk ends at the Plaza Isabel II, which is dominated by the Teatro Real.

Distance 1.2km (0.75 miles)
Time Half a day including visits
Start point Banco de España
✚ 19J 🚇 Banco de España
End point Teatro Real ✚ 16J
🚇 Opéra
Lunch/snack Círculo de Bellas Artes (€) ✉ Calle del Marqués de Casa Riera 2 ☎ 91 360 54 00

BEST THINGS TO DO

Peace and quiet

Around every corner in Madrid there is a bench or a small square to rest weary feet or eat a sandwich. In addition, the famous Parque del Retiro (➤ 52–53) is by no means the only green space in which to find peace and quiet.

Campo del Moro
Just below the Palacio Real, this park is more like a wood, even though the design is formal, with pleasant avenues and two attractive fountains – Las Conchas and Los Tritones. There are 70 different species of trees, some of which are over 150 years old.

Casa de Campo
To the west of the city, on the far side of the Río Manzanares, this vast park includes cafeterias, tennis courts, swimming pools, a lake, a zoo and the Parque de Atracciones (amusement park). The former hunting grounds are ideal for a picnic, kicking a ball around, or even tramping through the scrubland. During the Civil War, Franco's troops were based here, and some signs of the trenches are still visible. The most fun way to get there is by the Teleférico (➤ 148), but you can also go by Metro (Batán, Lago), or drive there.

BEST THINGS TO DO

Some parking places have become popular meeting spots for the gay community and prostitution is rife. It is best avoided at night.

Hotel Ritz
For a special treat, there is nothing quite like tea in the sheltered, flower-filled garden of one of the city's great hotels (➤ 126). It is a few steps north of the Prado (➤ 44–45).

Jardines de Sabatini
Just north of the Palacio Real, these formal gardens were only laid out in the 1930s. Few visitors come here, so peace and quiet are guaranteed for most of the day. Concerts are held here in the evenings in July and August.

Parque del Oeste
Set into the side of a hill, this rectangular park northwest of the Palacio Real has been renovated. The broad and elegant Paseo del Pintor Rosales runs along one side; the Ermita de San Antonio de la Florida (➤ 132) stands at the bottom of the slope. At the southern end is La Rosaleda, a rose garden which is at its best in May, and the Parque de la Montaña. Its temple was a gift from the Egyptian government. This is also the start of the Teleférico (➤ 148). The park is best avoided at night.

Plaza de Vázquez de Mella
North of the Gran Vía, near the Telefónica (➤ 148), this refurbished square has benches, a fountain and a small playground where youngsters can burn off surplus energy.

Real Jardín Botánico
A step away from the Prado and the *paseos*, this relaxing spot has stunning displays of flowers and shrubs (➤ 125). As this is still a centre for scientific research, don't expect cafeterias or refreshments for sale. The entrance is on the Plaza de Murillo.

Exploring

Around Old Madrid	81–112
Eastern Madrid	113–128
Northern Madrid	129–155

EXPLORING

Once regarded as a bastion of tradition, Madrid has discovered a new dynamism. It boasts tall glass-and-steel buildings, bustles with trendy shops and is undergoing a major pedestrianization of its old heart. Partially triggered by an ambitious (but unsuccessful) bid to host the 2012 Olympic Games, these and other changes reflect Spain's burgeoning economy. The international terminal at Barajas airport is breathtakingly contemporary, the three major art galleries have new additions, and the Metro system is constantly expanding. Yet ancient and modern seem to coexist happily. The larger shops may stay open at lunchtime, but some museums still close in the afternoon. Although international fast food outlets are common, century-old *tapas* bars are still crowded. As Archibald Lyall observed, back in the 1960s, Madrid is still the most Spanish and least Spanish city on the peninsula.

Around Old Madrid

Part of Madrid's great appeal is that medieval and modern stand elbow to elbow. Where else can you walk down a medieval street and, minutes later, admire one of the world's most famous modern paintings? Although there are traces of Arab influence from the time when Toledo was the Moorish capital of Spain, and Madrid a mere settlement, the heart of the city is essentially medieval.

It was only in 1561 that Felipe II decided to make Madrid his capital. And most of the grand buildings that we see today date from the 19th century. So, you can walk down a broad avenue, then turn a corner, go up an alleyway and find that you are treading on cobblestones centuries old.

Tall walls hide churches and monasteries that are entwined with the history of Spain. Small shops and wine bars still beat off supermarkets and fast-food restaurants, as locals combine tradition with their 21st-century lifestyles. Best explored on foot, this is a city where getting lost in the (safe) narrow lanes is part of the experience. Gather strength before you visit three of the world's great art galleries. Do as the locals do: sit on a bench in an old square, have a coffee, snack on tapas and watch the world go by. Madrid may be changing, but it isn't changing that fast.

EXPLORING

BASILICA DE SAN FRANCISCO EL GRANDE
The long-term renovation of this vast 18th-century church is complete. It stands on the site where San Francisco (St Francis of Assisi) is said to have stopped in 1217 on his pilgrimage to Santiago. It has served as a national pantheon and an army barracks; Joseph Bonaparte, the upstart king of Spain, wanted to use it as the parliament building. But, this remains a working church. The enormous dome measuring 33m (108ft) across is covered with 19th-century frescoes. In the first chapel to the left of the main entrance is *The Sermon of San Bernardino of Siena*

AROUND OLD MADRID

(1781) by Goya. He produced this unremarkable work at the age of 35, long before the dramatic canvases that are a highlight of the Prado (➤ 44–45). Even in his early career, Goya put himself into his paintings; here he is the one in yellow, on the right-hand side. Behind the altar is the Sala Capitular, with its carved wooden seats and paintings by 17th-century Spanish masters such as Francisco Zurbarán and Alonso Cano.

✚ 15L ✉ Calle de San Buenaventura 1 ☎ 91 365 38 00
🕓 Tue–Fri 11–12:30, 4–6:30, Sat 11–1:30 (in Aug Tue–Sun 11–12:30, 5–7:30). Closed public hols ✋ Inexpensive
🚇 Puerta de Toledo, La Latina

BASILICA DE SAN MIGUEL

One of Madrid's true baroque churches (1739–49), San Miguel was squeezed on to the small plot of ground that once held the church of San Justo. Architect Santiago Bonavía used several design tricks to give the interior the appearance of more space. In the narrow street, the exterior, with its elegant curved façade, statues and bells, also looks bigger. The consistency of the baroque design reflects Bonavía's Italian roots.

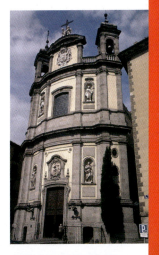

✚ 16K ✉ Calle de San Justo 4 ☎ 91 548 40 11 🕓 Jul to mid-Sep Mon–Fri 10:15–1, 6–9; public hols 9:45–1:45, 6–9; mid-Sep to Jun Mon–Fri 10:15–1, 6–9, public hols 9:45–1:45, 6:30–9:15 ✋ Free 🍴 Botín (➤ 84–85) 🚇 Sol, Opera, Tirso de Molina

EXPLORING

BOTÍN

Peer down the steps leading out of the southwest corner of the Plaza Mayor and you see what is, according to the *Guinness Book of Records*, the oldest restaurant business in the world. The descendants of Jean Botín, a French cook, ran a restaurant nearby on the Plaza de Herradores until fire destroyed the premises in the 1940s. The owner's nephews took over the present establishment, which dates back to 1725. Each dining-room reeks with atmosphere. One was the 16th-century *bodega* (wine cellar) and has arched brick walls; the others have dark beams and wall tiles. The focal point is the original *horno de asar* (wood-fired oven), hidden behind well-worn antique ceramic tiles. Although the inn has seen a few changes over the centuries, the oven has always been used to roast or bake meat. After three hours of slow cooking, the meat is so tender you can cut it with a fork. Legend has it that in 1765, the 19-year-old Goya worked at the original

AROUND OLD MADRID

Botín, washing dishes. Almost two centuries later, when Ernest Hemingway dined here, the typically *madrileño* dishes were much the same: stuffed pig's trotters, grilled fish and *cuajada* (curds). Not much has changed today.

www.restaurantebotin.es

🕀 16K ✉ Calle de los Cuchilleros 17 ☎ 91 366 42 17
🕒 Daily 1–4, 8–12 🚇 Sol, Tirso de Molina ❓ Reservation recommended

CASA MUSEO DE LOPE DE VEGA

Author of some 2,000 plays, Lope de Vega (1562–1635) was Spain's greatest playwright, penning an estimated 21 million lines. Capable of reading Latin at five, he wrote his first four-act play at the age of 12. This indefatigable genius also enlisted in the Spanish Navy (the Armada), was personal secretary to four aristocrats and had several wives and many children. Although he decided to become a priest in 1614, this had little effect on his love life. Lope lived in this house for the last 25 years of his life, and although only a few items are believed to be his, the author's detailed will enabled experts to refurnish the house much as he knew it.

The garden and vegetable patch of this two-storey, half-timbered shrine have been restored to fit a description in one of his poems: two trees, 10 flowers, two vines, an orange tree and a musk rose. Over the front door is the lintel found when cleaning out the well. The inscription reads *Parva propria magna, magna aliena parva* (To me, my small home is big; to me, other people's large homes are small). On a guided tour, as well as finding out about one of Spain's most renowned authors, you also get some idea of everyday life in a well-off family home in the early 17th century. Note the women's sitting-room where cushions are spread on the *estrado*, a small, Moorish-style dais.

🕀 19K ✉ Calle Cervantes 11 ☎ 91 429 92 16 🕒 Tue–Fri 9:30–2, Sat 10–2. Closed public hols, Aug 💰 Inexpensive. Free Sat 🚇 Antón Martín ❓ Guided tour only

CASA DE LA VILLA

Madrid's town hall sits on the Plaza de la Villa, which was a Moorish market place in the 10th and 11th centuries. In this cramped square it is difficult to appreciate the spiked towers and handsome façade that are so typical of 17th-century baroque-Castilian style. The balcony overlooking the Calle Mayor was added in 1789 so that Queen María of Parma could have a better view of the Corpus Christi procession. Opposite the town hall is the oldest surviving private house in Madrid, the 15th-century Casa y Torre de Lujanes. Part Gothic and part Moorish in style, this building is now used by academics. Legend has it that François I of France was imprisoned in the tower after his capture at the Battle of Pavia (1525).

On the south side of the sloping square is the Casa de Cisneros, built by a relative of the powerful Cardinal Cisneros in 1537. Note the façade, which is decorated in the plateresque style, so-called because the intricate carving looks like the work of a *platero* (silversmith). Remodelled in the early 1900s, today it makes an elegant office building for city employees. In the centre of the plaza stands a statue of the great Spanish admiral, the Marqués de Santa Cruz, victor over the Turks at the Battle of Lepanto (1571). The Casa de la Villa is only open to visitors once a week for a guided tour (Mon 5pm), which is strictly for enthusiasts.

www.munimadrid.es

✚ 16J ✉ Plaza de la Villa 5 ☎ 91 588 10 00 ✋ Free
Ⓜ Opera, La Latina, Sol

AROUND OLD MADRID

CATEDRAL DE LA ALMUDENA
Dedicated to the Virgin of Almudena, Madrid's most important church occupies the same hilltop site as the Palacio Real. The Catedral de la Almudena was designed by the Marques de Cubas in 1879, but work did not start until 1882 after the plans were changed to resemble a 13th-century cathedral similar to the one at Rheims. The building was eventually completed in the 1980s by architects Fernando Chueca Goitia and Carlos Sidro, who brought a neoclassical influence to the design. The cathedral was finally consecrated by Pope John Paul II in 1993.

In May 2004 the lofty Gothic nave provided a splendid setting for the wedding of the heir to the Spanish throne, Prince Felipe and Doña Letitia Ortiz Rocasolano, a former TV news presenter.

✚ 15J ✉ Calle de Bailén 10 ☎ 91 542 22 00 🕐 Daily 9–9
✋ Free 🚇 Opera

COLEGIATA DE SAN ISIDRO
The bulky twin towers of this cathedral were designed to emphasize the importance of the church that is dedicated to Madrid's patron saint. Built between 1622 and 1633, the interior is in the shape of a cross, with the dome above the transept.

After Carlos III expelled the Jesuits in 1767, he commissioned the noted architect Ventura Rodríguez to remodel the gloomy interior. For over 200 years, the remains of San Isidro and Santa María de la Cabeza, his equally holy wife, have been venerated here.

✚ 17K ✉ Calle de Toledo 37 ☎ 91 369 20 37
🕐 Daily 8–12, 6:30–8:30. Closed during services
✋ Free 🚇 La Latina, Tirso de Molina

EXPLORING

CONVENTO DE LAS CARBONERAS
It is difficult to find this convent. From Plaza de la Villa, step into Calle del Codo and the door is on the right. The nuns belong to a closed order known as the Carboneras (coal cellars), because their painting of the Virgin Mary was found in a coal cellar. The convent is better known in Madrid for selling home-made *dulces* (biscuits) and sweetmeats. This tradition dates back to the 16th century when Santa Teresa of Avila distributed treats made from sugar and egg yolk to the poor. Ring a bell for service; an elaborate serving hatch ensures that the privacy of the nuns is not disturbed.

✚ 16J ✉ Plaza Conde de Miranda 3 ☎ 91 548 37 01 🕐 Mon–Fri 9:30–1, 4–6:30 🚇 Sol

IGLESIA DE LAS CALATRAVAS
In the 17th and 18th centuries the most important street in Madrid was the Calle de Alcalá, which led to the university town of Alcalá de Henares. Facing today's traffic and hemmed in by office buildings, this church is all that is left of the original 17th-century convent of the military order of the Comendadoras of Calatrava, founded by the wives of knights who joined the Crusades. Topped by a fine dome, the massive pink-brick exterior is covered in ornate sculpture. The interior is even more opulent. Here, the focal point in the gloomy light is the massive altarpiece of

José Churriguera, the sculptor who lent his name to an exuberant baroque decorative style – Churrigueresque.
🚌 18J ✉ Calle de Alcalá 25 ☎ 91 521 80 35 🕐 Half hour before Mass (8, 12, 1; Sun 11, 12, 1 and 7) ✋ Free 🍴 Círculo de Bellas Artes (€) Ⓜ Sevilla

IGLESIA DE SAN ANDRÉS APÓSTOL

San Andrés is a church with two significant chapels. San Andrés itself, occupying the domed end of the building, reopened in 1998 after years of renovation. Compared with the poorly-lit interiors of most churches, this one is a surprise: bright pink and grey, highlighted with fruit, flowers and angels, like the marzipan on an expensive cake. At the back of San Andrés is the Capilla de San Isidro, which once held the bones of San Isidro, Madrid's patron saint. Beneath the church, renovation continues on the 16th-century Capilla del Obispo (Bishop's Chapel). Closed to the public for restoration, it contains one of the most magnificent Gothic altarpieces in Madrid, a towering, gilded masterpiece attributed to Francisco Giralte.
🚌 15K ✉ Plaza de San Andrés 1 ☎ 91 365 48 71 🕐 Mon–Sat 8–12:30, 6–8, Sun 9–2 ✋ Free Ⓜ La Latina

EXPLORING

IGLESIA Y CONVENTO DE LAS TRINITARIAS

The Trinitarias, who wear white cassocks marked with a bold red and blue cross, are a closed order of nuns. In their 17th-century church a plaque commemorates the burial place of Cervantes, author of *Don Quixote*. Each year on 23 April, a memorial service for Spain's most famous writer is held by Spain's Academy of Language. Authors Lope de Vega, Luis de Góngora and Francisco de Quevedo also lived nearby and worshipped here. Although the church has fine paintings and a grand altarpiece, the appeal here is to follow in the footsteps of these literary giants. Visiting hours are limited to half an hour before mass, but you are not required to stay for the service itself.

✚ 19K ✉ Calle de Lope de Vega 18 ☎ 91 429 56 71 ⊕ Mon–Fri 8:30am, Sat 7pm, Sun 9:30am, 11:30am ✋ Free 🚇 Antón Martín, Sevilla

MERCADO ANTÓN MARTÍN

The once-popular Mercado de San Miguel (Plaza de San Miguel) has fallen on hard times, but, you can get a taster of what locals like to buy and eat at the Mercado Antón Martín. A stroll through the two floors of stalls shows why Madrid is called Spain's 'biggest port': all the best freshly caught fish comes straight to the capital. *Mero* (halibut) and *rape* (hake) glisten; shellfish are piled high. Then there are the *charcuterías* (delicatessens) with dozens of types of sausages and cheeses. Skeins of dried peppers decorate the fruit and vegetable stands; butchers wielding crescent-shaped cleavers slice expensive cuts of pork and beef, as well as cheaper tripe and offal.

The *frutos secos* stand has every sort of dried fruit and nut, pasta and olive you can imagine. New are stalls selling organic foods and

AROUND OLD MADRID

natural cosmetics, as well as the little cafés run by Peruvian immigrants, who serve up South American dishes such as *ceviche* (marinated seafood) and *papas rellenas* (fried stuffed potatoes). If you venture up to the top floor of the market, you will find the **Centro Amor de Dios,** a school dedicated to all things flamenco: dancing, singing and guitar playing.

🕂 18K

Mercado Antón Martín

✉ Calle de Santa Isabel 5 ✋ Free Ⓜ Antón Martín

Centro Amor de Dios

✉ Above Mercado Antón Martín ☎ 91 360 04 34 Ⓜ Antón Martín

EXPLORING

MONASTERIO DE LAS DESCALZAS REALES
Best places to see, pages 36–37.

MONASTERIO DE LA ENCARNACÍON

Another of Madrid's closed orders dedicated to the royal family, this convent is famous on two counts: its collection of some 4,000 *relicarios* (reliquaries) and an annual miracle. Whether you believe that the reliquaries contain the authentic bones of saints or a fragment of the true cross depends on your religious persuasion. However, according to the curator, visitors should appreciate the reliquaries as works of art, created as expressions of religious belief during the 17th century – Spain's Golden Age.

The reliquaries are preserved in glass cases, which line the walls of what looks like a heavily decorated library with an impressive, gilded altar. They come in all shapes and sizes in precious materials of the period, such as coral, marble and crystal, as well as gold and silver. One of the most venerated reliquaries is a small vial containing a droplet of blood, which is reputedly from the 4th-century physician and martyr, San Pantaleón. On 26 July, the eve of the saint's feast day, the vial is placed on the altar of the church in the convent. There, according to the faithful, *la sangre* (the blood) rematerializes. The convent, still home to a small community of nuns, was founded in 1611 by Margarita of Austria, wife of Felipe III. Although the handsome façade is original, architect Ventura Rodríguez remodelled the interior after a fire in the 18th century.

www.patrimonionacional.es

✚ 15H ✉ Plaza de la Encarnación 1 ☎ 91 454 88 00 🕒 Tue–Sat 10:30–12:45, 4–5:45, Sun, public hols 11–1:45. Closed Fri pm, Mon ✋ Inexpensive; free Wed for EU citizens 🚇 Opera ❓ Joint ticket available with the nearby Monasterio de las Descalzas Reales (▶ 36–37)

AROUND OLD MADRID

EXPLORING

MUSEO NACIONAL CENTRO DE ARTE REINA SOFÍA
Best places to see, pages 42–43.

MUSEO DE LA REAL ACADEMIA DE BELLAS ARTES DE SAN FERNANDO
Both Picasso and Dalí studied at the grand but grim-looking Royal Academy, the oldest museum in the city (1752). Climb the sombre, massive stone steps; once inside the gallery, all is brightly lit. This uncrowded museum has a serendipitous charm. Although Goya's paintings are at the end of the itinerary, don't rush there but take your time to discover Francisco Zurbarán's powerful portraits of monks, which dominate Room 6, and Rubens'

AROUND OLD MADRID

Susana y Los Viejos (Susanna and the Elders), the highlight of Room 13. There are curiosities galore, such as Giuseppe Archimboldo's curious painting in Room 14. Called *La Primavera (Spring)*, this is a portrait concocted from daisies, wild strawberries, roses and iris. Two contrasting portraits of famous generals, Napoleon Bonaparte and George Washington, dominate Room 35. The French emperor seems to be wearing a dress, while the American holds a map of the capital named after him.

Find Joaquín Sorolla (➤ 46–47) and Juan Gris among a mish-mash of modern Spanish artists in Rooms 25 and 29. Room 20 is popular for its famous but surprisingly small Goya painting, *El Entierro de la Sardina (The Burial of the Sardine)*, depicting this rather bizarre local custom which still takes place. On Ash Wednesday, a mock funeral procession – bearing a tiny coffin and accompanied by a jazz band – makes its way from the Ermita de San Antonio de la Florida (➤ 132) to the Los Pajaritos fountain in the Casa de Campo, where the sardine is interred. Other works by Goya include self-portraits, as well as sketches for the famous oils of scenes in a madhouse, of the Inquisition and of penitents.

http://rabasf.insde.es

✚ 18J ✉ Calle de Alcalá 13 ☎ 91 524 08 64 🕒 Tue–Fri 9–7, Sat–Mon, public hols 9–2:30 (some rooms closed from time to time) 💰 Inexpensive; free under-18s, over-65s, Wed 🚇 Sevilla, Sol

MUSEO THYSSEN-BORNEMISZA
Best places to see, pages 48–49.

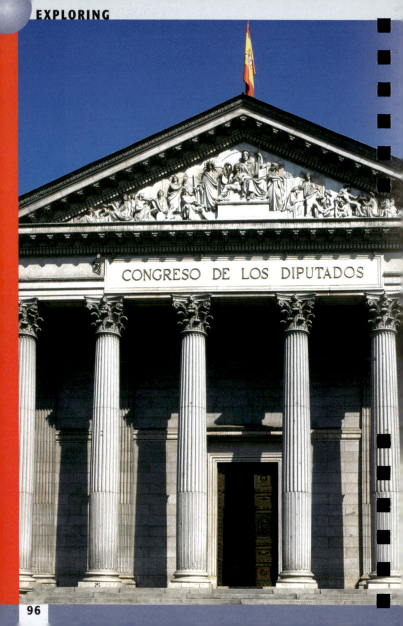

AROUND OLD MADRID

PALACIO DE LAS CORTES

The events of 23 February 1981 marked a turning point in Spanish history. Civil Guard commander Colonel Tejero entered the *Salón de Sesiones* in the parliament building, firing his pistol and ordering delegates to the floor. Television cameras relayed the action live to a shocked country and for a while it looked as if Spain might revert to military dictatorship. Discussion of those events are the prime topic during the 30- to 45-minute tours of this neo-classical mid-19th century building. First, however, you pass through four rooms with ornate paintings, chandeliers and furniture. There are portraits of 19th-century politicians and an intriguing 3m-high (10ft) clock that registers the weather and humidity, as well as the date and time. Spaniards study the seven constitutions of Spain – from the earliest (1812), to the current one issued in 1978 and signed by Juan Carlos.

The highlight, however, is the deputies' chamber with its 350 leather armchairs. The order of seating for the cabinet reflects the seniority of the ministry; two panels show how individual members vote: *sí*, *no* or *abs*. But what Spaniards of all ages want to know is, 'where are the bullet holes?' Even bored teenagers pay attention as the guide points out the 40 punctures in the walls and ceiling. Parents recall those momentous hours when tanks threatened Valencia, and Spain waited to see whether or not the new democracy would survive.

www.congreso.es

✚ 19J ✉ Plaza de las Cortes s/n ☎ 91 390 60 00 🕐 Sat 10:30–12:30, guided tour only every 30 mins. Closed Aug, public hols Ⓜ Sevilla, Banco de España ✋ Free ❓ Official ID (such as a passport) required, free booklet given

PALACIO REAL
Best places to see, pages 50–51.

PLAZA MAYOR
Best places to see, pages 54–55.

EXPLORING

a walk around medieval Madrid

Start at the Plaza Mayor (➤ 54–55). The steps at the southwest corner lead to the Calle de los Cuchilleros, with its centuries-old mesones (taverns). Cross Plaza de la Puerta Cerrada to Calle de la Cava Baja.

At No 9, La Posada de la Villa dates back to 1642. This district retains its historic atmosphere, with tiny shops that still sell basketware and *alpargatas* (rope-soled sandals). At the end, across the Plaza del Humilladero, on the right, is the huge dome of Iglesia de San Andrés (➤ 89).

Walk round the south side and into the Plaza de la Paja.

Once the main square of the medieval city, this was overlooked by a royal palace. Today, a lone statue sits on a bench reading the paper.

At the bottom of the square turn right along Calle del Príncipe de Anglona to the 15th-century Iglesia de San Pedro el Viejo, marked by a 14th-century mudéjar (Moorish) tower. Turn left on Travesía del Nuncio and right onto Calle de Segovia.

A plaque at No 1 records the birthplace of San Isidro, Madrid's patron saint. Turn immediately left on Calle del Doctor Letamendi, past the Basilica de San Miguel (➤ 83), along Calle de Puñonrostro and Calle del Codo. Pass the Convento de las Carboneras on the left (➤ 88). Continue to the town hall, the Casa de la Villa (➤ 86).

AROUND OLD MADRID

Turn right, walk back along the Calle Mayor to the Plaza Mayor.

Distance 2km (1.2 miles)
Time Half a day with stops
Start/end point Plaza Mayor ✚ 16J 🚇 Sol
Lunch La Posada de la Villa (➤ 59)

EXPLORING

PUERTA DEL SOL

Streets radiate in all directions from this oblong plaza, one of the focal points of Madrid. Dominating all he surveys is Carlos III (1759–88) astride a horse and usually with a pigeon perched on his royal head. The words on the plinth are a paean of praise to the king, who is regarded as 'the best mayor of Madrid'. He looks across at the Casa de Correos, the post office from 1766–1847. To the right of the main entrance, a plaque honours the heroes of the 2 de mayo, the rebellion on 2 May 1808 against the French army that had occupied the capital. Set in the pavement (sidewalk) in front of the Casa de Correos, another plaque marks Kilometre 0, the *Origen de las Carreteras Radiales*. This is the

point from which all distances to and from Madrid are measured. The Casa de Correos clock is an integral part of Spain's New Year celebrations. As it strikes midnight, Spaniards all over

AROUND OLD MADRID

the country watch television and eat *las uvas de la suerte* (lucky grapes), gulping down one grape per chime to ensure good fortune in the new year. Other statues in this square include *La Mariblanca*, next to the station, and the emblem of Madrid – the famous *oso* (bear) standing on his hind legs and eating fruit from the *madroño* (madrona tree). It's behind the Carlos III statue.
✚ 17J 🚇 Sol ❓ Crammed on New Year's Eve. Works in the square for the foreseeable future

PUERTA DE TOLEDO
How are the mighty fallen! In 1808, when Frenchman Joseph Bonaparte was installed as king of Spain by his brother Napoleon, he gave orders for a triumphal arch to be erected at the Toledo gate. After Joseph was ousted by Fernando VII in 1814, work continued on the arch, but the triumph it celebrated was the Spanish defeat of the French! Another triumphal arch, the Puerta de Alcalá, is also lost in traffic, at the northwest corner of the Parque del Retiro. A symbol of Madrid, this is best appreciated at night, when it is tastefully floodlit.
✚ 15M

EXPLORING

EL RASTRO

Sunday would not be Sunday without a visit to the Rastro Flea Market. This sprawl of stalls attracts as many locals as visitors, even if they have no intention of buying anything. Start at the Plaza de Cascorro, with its statue of El Cascorro (Eloy Gonzalo), a 19th-century hero of the Spanish-American war in Cuba. The stalls here sell leather bags, clothing and perfumes of dubious origin. Once you reach the trees that shade Calle de la Ribera de Curtidores, the quality improves, with shops making solid furniture and wrought-iron weather vanes. Bars and pastry shops along the street are also open. In a courtyard, through an ancient arch, is the Galerías Piquer, a complex of 50 antiques shops selling everything from clocks to Oriental furniture.

Explore side streets such as Calle de San Cayetano, Calle de Rodas and Calle de Fray Ceferino González, for art equipment and picture frames, bird cages and fishing nets.

16L ✉ Calle de Ribera de Curtidores ⊙ Sun, public hols am 🚇 La Latina, Puerta de Toledo

AROUND OLD MADRID

HOTELS

El Antiguo Convento (€€€)
This refurbished 17th-century convent has tastefully decorated rooms overlooking the cloisters and a tranquil garden. Expensive, but well worth the outlay for a special stay.
✉ Calle de las Monjas, Boadilla del Monte ☎ 91 632 22 20; www.elconvento.net 🚌 571, 573

Casa de Madrid (€€€)
A small exclusive bed-and-breakfast, facing the Royal Opera House. The rooms in the 18th-century building are individually furnished with portraits and antique furniture. A special experience.
✉ Calle Arrieta 2 ☎ 91 559 57 91; www.casademadrid.com 🚇 Opera

Hotel Asturias (€–€€)
Over 100 years old, this 170-room hotel is good for bargain accommodation in the middle of the city.
✉ Calle de Sevilla 2 ☎ 91 429 66 76; www.chh.es 🚇 Sevilla

Hotel Emperador (€€€)
With 241 rooms right in the middle of town, this is popular with package tour organizers, but the rooms are spacious and there is the bonus of a roof-top pool.
✉ Gran Vía 53 ☎ 91 547 28 00, fax 91 547 28 17; www.emperadorhotel.com 🚇 Gran Vía

Hotel Moderno (€€)
This 3-star hotel is only moments from the Plaza Mayor and the Puerta del Sol. Families welcome.
✉ Calle del Arenal 2 ☎ 91 531 09 00; www.hotel-moderno.com 🚇 Sol

Hotel Opera (€€–€€€)
A stylish, contemporary 3-star hotel handy for the Teatro Real, the Palacio Real (➤ 50–51) and the old quarter. Public parking nearby.
✉ Cuesta de Santo Domingo 2 ☎ 91 541 28 00; www.hotelopera.com 🚇 Opera

Hotel Palace (€€€)
Built in 1913, this Westin 5-star hotel lives up to its name, from the stained-glass dome over the huge lobby to the gym, garage, two restaurants and over 400 rooms. A short walk from Madrid's three famous art museums.
✉ Plaza de las Cortes 7 ☎ 91 360 80 00; www.westinpalacemadrid.com
🚇 Banco de España

Hotel Suecia (€€€)
Practical rather than pretty, the Suecia has 128 modern rooms and a seventh-floor terrace for sunbathing.
✉ Calle del Marqués de Casa Riera 4 ☎ 91 531 69 00; www.hotelsuecia.com 🚇 Banco de España

ME Madrid Reina Victoria (€€€)
You can't miss the ornate tower of this trendy hotel that overlooks the bars and cafés of the Plaza de Santa Ana. The 192 rooms are funky, with high-tech conveniences.
✉ Plaza de Santa Ana 14 ☎ 91 701 60 00; www.mebymelia.com 🚇 Sol

RESTAURANTS

El Asador de Aranda (€€€)
One of seven Madrid branches of this popular chain of restaurants. Try the regional speciality of Castile: lamb roasted slowly in a wood-fired oven.
✉ Calle Preciados 44 ☎ 91 547 21 56 🕐 Lunch, dinner. Closed Mon dinner
🚇 Callao, Santo Domingo

La Bola (€€)
Behind the Plaza del Oriente, this is the sort of place where locals bring their out-of-town friends for authentic *cocido madrileño* (Madrid stew). Open since 1870; no credit cards.
✉ Calle de la Bola 5 ☎ 91 547 69 30 🕐 Lunch, dinner. Closed Sun dinner
🚇 Santo Domingo, Opera

Botín (€€)
See pages 84–85.

AROUND OLD MADRID

La Broche (€€€)
La Broche is the domain of master chef Sergi Arola, who has won every plaudit going in the last few years, including two Michelin stars. The cuisine is Mediterranean, with a Catalan twist.
✉ Miguel Angel 29–31 ☎ 91 399 34 37 🕐 Lunch, dinner. Closed Sat–Sun and public hols Ⓜ Gregorio Marañon

El Buey (€€€)
Its name means ox, and beef is the speciality, with prime cuts. There are alternative fish dishes. Booking is essential.
✉ Plaza de la Marina Española 1 ☎ 91 541 30 41 🕐 Lunch, dinner. Closed Sun dinner and public hols Ⓜ Opera, Santo Domingo

La Cabaña (€€–€€€)
Charcoal-grilled steaks are the speciality of this pricey, but reliable Argentinian restaurant, not far from Sol. Tables are in great demand, especially on weekends, so booking is essential.
✉ Ventura de la Vega 10 ☎ 91 420 17 41 🕐 Lunch, dinner Ⓜ Sevilla

Café de la Opera (€€)
Right by the Teatro Real opera house. The waiters and waitresses are opera students, who serve and sing opera and *zarzuela* (light opera). International dishes.
✉ Calle de Arrieta 6 ☎ 91 542 63 82 🕐 Dinner only Ⓜ Opera

Casa Gallega (€€€)
Galician restaurants specialize in seafood. Try *sopa de mariscos* (fish soup) or *cogote de merluza* (hake baked in the oven).
✉ Calle de Bordadores 11 ☎ 91 541 90 55 🕐 Lunch, dinner Ⓜ Sol, Opera

Casa Lucio (€€€)
Popular with the royal family, foreign politicians and film stars. A fashionable but affordable restaurant on Madrid's restaurant row that is known for Castilian dishes such as stews and roasts. Booking essential.
✉ Calle de la Cava Baja 35 ☎ 91 365 32 52 🕐 Lunch, dinner. Sat dinner only. Closed Aug and public hols Ⓜ La Latina

EXPLORING

A'Casiña (€€€)
See page 59.

El Cenador del Prado (€€–€€€)
When you want to try contemporary Spanish cuisine, this is one of the best. Near the Plaza Santa Ana. To enjoy the best of the Heranz brothers, try the *menú de degustación* (special tasting menu).
✉ Calle del Prado 4 ☎ 91 429 15 61 🕒 Lunch, dinner. Closed Sun, 1 week mid-Aug 🚇 Antón Martín, Sevilla

La Chata (€€€)
Reputed to be a favourite among bullfighters, the menu features roast suckling pig, lamb and langoustines with sherry sauce or wild mushrooms. Good *tapas* and wines by the glass.
✉ Cava de la Baja 24 ☎ 91 366 14 58 🕒 Lunch, dinner. Closed Tue, Wed lunch 🚇 La Latina

Las Cuevas de Luis Candelas (€€–€€€)
Just off the Plaza Mayor, this traditional tavern offers Castilian dishes, especially roast lamb and pork. Touristy but fun, with plenty of locals, especially for Sunday lunch.
✉ Calle de los Cuchilleros 1 ☎ 91 366 54 28 🕒 Lunch, dinner 🚇 Sol, Tirso de Molina

El Estragón (€–€€)
Vegetarian restaurants are still thin on the ground in Madrid. El Estragón has a great location, a relaxed ambience and offers veggie standards like stir-fried vegetables and mushroom lasagne.
✉ Plaza de la Paja 10 ☎ 91 365 89 82 🕒 12:30pm–12:30am 🚇 La Latina

Lhardy (€€€)
In 1839, the author of *Carmen* persuaded Emile Lhardy to open this French restaurant and it is still going strong. Beautiful, historic and expensive: pheasant with grapes, sole in champagne sauce.
✉ Carrera de San Jerónimo 8 ☎ 91 521 33 85 🕒 Lunch, dinner. Closed Sun, public hols dinner 🚇 Sevilla, Sol

AROUND OLD MADRID

Malacatín (€–€€)
Despite its echoes of the Franco era, this is still a friendly little spot near the Rastro Flea Market. Another favourite with locals who order *cocido* (Madrid stew).
✉ Calle de la Ruda 5 ☎ 91 365 52 41 🕐 Lunch, dinner. Closed Sat dinner, Sun, public hols, Aug Ⓜ La Latina, Tirso de Molina

La Posada de la Villa (€€–€€€)
See page 59.

Mi Pueblo (€€)
Excellent value traditional home cooking *(cocina casera)* is available here. The menu includes a small selection of meat and fish dishes and there's wine from Arganda del Rey.
✉ Costanilla de Santiago 2 ☎ 91 548 20 73 🕐 Closed Sun eve, Mon Ⓜ Opera, Sol

Taberna de Antonio Sánchez (€–€€)
Named in honour of the bullfighter Antonio Sánchez, and founded by his father. *Aficionados* meet below the bull's head mounted on the wall of the oldest tavern (1830) in Madrid.
✉ Calle Mesón de Paredes 13 ☎ 91 539 78 26 🕐 Lunch, dinner. Closed Sun dinner Ⓜ Tirso de Molina

La Trucha (€–€€)
Specializing in Andalucian dishes in general and trout in particular, this is the sister restaurant of the *tapas* bar of the same name. Both are just off the Plaza de Santa Ana.
✉ Calle de Núñez de Arce 6 ☎ 91 532 08 82 🕐 Lunch, dinner. Closed Sun, Mon, Aug Ⓜ Sol, Sevilla

Viuda de Vacas (€€)
Home-style Castilian cooking, from oxtail to tripe, is the speciality of this oak-beamed restaurant with its wood oven.
✉ Calle de la Cava Alta 23 ☎ 91 366 58 47 🕐 Lunch, dinner. Closed Sun dinner, Thu, public hols, Aug Ⓜ La Latina

SHOPPING

ANTIQUES, BOOKS AND MUSIC
Felix Antigüedades
This antiques dealer in the heart of the Rastro flea market specializes in Oriental art, objets d'art after 1700 and musical instruments.
✉ Plaza General Vara del Rey 3 ☎ 91 528 48 30 Ⓜ La Latina

Félix Manzanero
Manzanero served an apprenticeship with the legendary José Ramirez and now has his own shop, where both professionals and amateurs come to buy handcrafted instruments. He also has on display antique guitars, dating back to the 18th century.
✉ Calle de Santa Ana 12 ☎ 91 366 00 47 Ⓜ La Latina, Tirso de Molina

Galerías Piquer
Most of the score of antique shops that overlook the quiet courtyard have old-fashioned, rather heavy Spanish antiques. Go during the week to avoid the crowds on a Sunday.
✉ Calle de Ribera de Curtidores 29 Ⓜ La Latina, Puerta de Toledo

Manuel Gonzáles Contreras
There's a waiting list for custom-built guitars, but you may find what you're looking for in Manuel Gonzáles Contrera's workshop. Classical guitarist, Andres Segovia was one of his clients.
✉ Calle Mayor 80 ☎ 91 542 2201 Ⓜ Sol

Petra's International Bookshop
This is a treasure trove of mostly second-hand books in every category you can think of and in half a dozen different languages.
✉ Calle de Campomanes 13 ☎ 91 541 72 91 Ⓜ Santo Domingo

ARTS, CRAFTS, GIFTS AND DESIGN
El Angel
Spain is known for its shops selling religious items, from pictures of saints to nuns' habits. El Angel is one of the best.
✉ Calle de Esparteros 3 ☎ 91 532 04 91 Ⓜ Sol

AROUND OLD MADRID

El Arco Artesanía
In the heart of the tourist district, this building houses 30 or more craftsmen and women, producing contemporary jewellery, textiles and ceramics. Well priced and well worth a look.
✉ Plaza Mayor 9 ☎ 91 365 26 80 Ⓜ Sol

Cántaro
Spanish pottery and ceramics make good souvenirs and presents. This shop near the Gran Vía has a wide range, representing every corner of Spain. The only difficulty is making a choice!
✉ Calle de la Flor Baja 8 ☎ 91 547 95 14 Ⓜ Santo Domingo, Plaza de España

Casa Jiménez
Spanish *mantillas* may not be a practical gift for visitors from foreign countries, but *mantonas* (shawls) can make attractive presents. The shawls here are often described as works of art.
✉ Calle de Preciados 42 ☎ 91 548 05 26 Ⓜ Callao

María José Fermín
In addition to barbecues, chairs and tables, this traditional wrought-iron worker makes attractive weather vanes adorned with cockerels and witches.
✉ Ribera de Curtidores 9 ☎ 91 539 43 67 Ⓜ La Latina

Museo Thyssen-Bornemisza
Down in the museum's gift shop is a wide choice of reproductions of the most famous paintings in the museum. Best sellers include Gauguin's hot-coloured South Pacific scene, *Mata Mua* (1892); find it on everything from expensive silk scarves to simple posters.
✉ Paseo del Prado 8 ☎ 91 369 01 51 Ⓜ Banco de España

Pérez A Fernández
It's worth going to this century-old silversmiths, just to look at the exterior of this beautiful shop. Inside, the handcrafted silver is based on traditional Galician designs.
✉ Calle de Zaragoza 3 ☎ 91 366 42 79 Ⓜ Opera

EXPLORING

FOOD AND DRINK
Casa Mira
Turrón (nougat) is the national confectionery of Spain, and comes in a wide variety of flavours. This shop is owned by the descendants of a *turrón*-maker from Alicante, who brought his special recipe to Madrid in the 19th century. The mixture of almonds and honey is still made by hand.
✉ Carrera de San Jerónimo 30 ☎ 91 429 67 96 🚇 Sevilla

La Mallorquina
This cake shop, which has a second branch, has been a feature of the Puerta del Sol since 1894. Locals come to buy biscuits and buns, chocolates, sweets and cakes for a special occasion.
✉ Puerta del Sol 8/ Calle Mayor 2 ☎ 91 521 12 01 🚇 Sol

El Palacio de los Quesos
The Palace of Cheeses has all the Spanish specialities. Manchego, for example, is available *tierno* (young) to *añejo* (mature). Try *cabrales*, a blue-veined, full-flavoured mixture of goat and sheeps' milk cheese from Asturias.
✉ Calle Mayor 53 ☎ 91 548 16 23 🚇 Sol, Opera

Tutti-Frutti
José Rodriguez's family business offers an exotic selection of ice creams including flavours like Philadelphia cream cheese with honey. One of seven branches in Madrid.
✉ Puerto del Sol 5 ☎ 91 522 93 88 🚇 Sol

ENTERTAINMENT
BARS, CLUBS AND LIVE MUSIC
Berlin Cabaret
Since the classy German cabaret singer Ute Lemper appeared in Madrid a few years ago, there's been no looking back. This bar and club, in the increasingly chic La Latina district, attracts international as well as home-grown artists.
✉ Costanilla de San Pedro 11 ☎ 91 366 20 34 🕐 Shows from 11pm daily. Closed Sun 🚇 La Latina

AROUND OLD MADRID

Café Central
Arguably Madrid's best-known jazz café. The elegant decoration includes a carved wood ceiling and pictures made of leaded, coloured glass. Features artists from the USA and Europe.
✉ Plaza del Angel 10 ☎ 91 369 41 43 🕓 1pm–2:30am; weekends to 3:30am Ⓜ Sol, Antón Martín

Café de Chinitas
Enthusiastic audiences are mainly Spanish, though foreigners are also fans of flamenco. This restaurant, set in the basement of a 17th-century palace, has nightly shows starting at 10:30pm.
✉ Calle de Torija 7 ☎ 91 559 51 35 or 91 547 15 02 🕓 9pm–dawn. Closed Sun Ⓜ Santo Domingo

Las Carboneras
A club run by young flamenco enthusiasts and performers.
✉ Plaza del Conde de Miranda 1 ☎ 91 542 86 77 🕓 9–midnight. Closed Sun Ⓜ Sol, Opera

Casa Patas
This popular flamenco nightclub, highly regarded by locals for its classy performers, doubles as a restaurant and *tapas* bar.
✉ Calle Cañizares 10 ☎ 91 369 04 96 🕓 Noon–5, 8pm–2am; Fri, Sat 8pm–3am. Closed Sun. Shows 10.30pm Mon–Thu, 9pm–11pm, 12am–2am Fri–Sat Ⓜ Antón Martín, Tirso de Molina

Los Gabrieles (€)
No point in looking for a sign; listen for the flamenco. Century-old hand-painted wall tiles depict scenes from *Don Quixote*.
✉ Calle de Echegaray 17 ☎ 91 429 6261 🕓 Mon–Sat 1pm–3am, Sun 9pm–5am Ⓜ Sevilla, Sol

Joy Madrid
The lovely old Teatro Eslava (1872) now hosts Madrid's hottest nightclub.
✉ Calle de Arenal 11 ☎ 91 366 37 33 (after 11pm) 🕓 11:30pm–closing; Fri–Sun 6:30pm–closing Ⓜ Sol

EXPLORING

Palacio Gaviria
The handsome 19th-century mansion plays host to a variety of music in a dozen surprisingly elegant rooms. Dress code is more formal, prices are justifiably high.
✉ Calle de Arenal 9 ☎ 91 526 60 69 🕐 Mon–Wed 11am–4am, Thu–Sat 11am–5:30am, Sun 8:30pm–2am 🚇 Sol

La Riviera
If you are young and love big, live rock concerts, then this is definitely the best place to go in the city.
✉ Paseo Virgen del Puerto ☎ 91 365 24 15 🕐 Tue–Sun noon–6am 🚇 Puerto del Angel

THEATRE, MUSIC AND DANCE
Teatro Monumental
This auditorium is the home of the orchestra of Spain's national television station. The season runs from October to April. There are also performances of *zarzuela* and opera.
✉ Calle de Atocha 65 ☎ 91 429 12 81 🕐 Box office: Tue–Fri 11–2, 5–7 🚇 Antón Martín

Teatro Real
The 1990s saw this theatre restored to its 1850s grandeur and it has now joined the ranks of Europe's great opera houses. The season runs from September to July; tickets can be difficult to come by. There are regular tours (Wed–Mon, tel 91 516 06 96).
✉ Plaza de Oriente ☎ 91 516 06 60 🕐 Box office 10–1:30, 5:30–8. Closed Sun. Tickets also from www.entradas.com 🚇 Opera

Teatro de la Zarzuela
Zarzuela is the light opera of Spain and Madrid is considered its home. Spanish light opera may not get the recognition that serious opera receives, but it is worth noting that Plácido Domingo, whose parents were *zarzuela* singers, has recorded popular songs in this style. The theatre, built in 1856, is a copy of La Scala in Milan.
✉ Calle de Jovellanos 4 ☎ 91 524 54 10 🕐 Box office 12–6. Tickets also from www.ticketcredit.com, www.servicaixa.com 🚇 Banco de España

Eastern Madrid

Begun in the 18th century and extended in the 19th century, the Paseos are broad boulevards that divide the old city from eastern Madrid. At 646m (2,200ft) above sea level, Madrid is the highest capital in Europe, with baking heat in high summer. The tree-lined *paseos*, small squares and large parks, such as the Retiro and the Jardín Botánico, are the lungs of the city.

Parque del Retiro

They are lined with grand buildings from Spain's days as a colonial power. As well as the three world-famous art galleries (the Prado, Thyssen-Bornemisza and Reina Sofia), there are museums dedicated to the navy (Museo Naval) and anthropology (Museo Nacional de Antropología).

The three major galleries are always clumped together under the heading of the Paseo del Arte. However, the richness, size and variety of art on display are too much to appreciate in a short time.

Break up visits with walks in the park, trips to other museums or just by strolling along the elegant boulevards. A tip: always give in to the temptation to stop for coffee and cake at an open-air café. It's what Madrid is all about.

EXPLORING

EASTERN MADRID

CASÓN DEL BUEN RETIRO
Works to this building are part of the enormous expansion project of the Prado (➤ 44–45). When it reopens, the museum's collection of 19th-century art will be housed in what is one of the few reminders of the grandeur that was once the Buen Retiro Palace, built for Philip IV in the 17th century. *Casón* usually means 'big house', but a century ago it was used as a pejorative term to describe the dilapidated structure. When this part of the Prado art complex reopens, it will house 19th-century art.
www.museoprado.es
✚ 20K ✉ Calle Alfonso XII 28, Calle Felipe IV 13 ☎ 91 330 28 00 🍴 Plenty nearby (€) Ⓜ Banco de España, Retiro Atocha ❓ Check the building progress on the website above

MUSEO NACIONAL DE ANTROPOLOGÍA
This would be dull were it not for the quirky objects on display. School children rush to the ghoulish Room III, to the left of the main entrance, to see the skeleton of the *Gigante Extremeño*, Spain's tallest man. Agustín Luengo Capilla, who died in 1849, aged 26, was an astonishing 2.35m (7.7ft) tall. Most of the building is devoted to tribal relics: big gods and little gods, wooden shields and dugout canoes. Other favourites include Brazilian feathered headdresses and shrunken heads dangling in a glass case.
http://mnantropologia.mcu.es
✚ 21L ✉ Calle Alfonso XII 68 ☎ 91 530 64 18 🕐 Tue–Sat 9:30–8, Sun, public hols 10–2 (Jul, Aug open until 10:30pm Thu) 🎟 Inexpensive; free EU citizens under 18, over 65; free to all Sat pm, Sun) 🚆 Atocha RENFE

115

MUSEO NACIONAL DE ARTES DECORATIVAS

Like London's Victoria and Albert Museum and the Musée des Arts Decoratifs in Paris, this is a must for anyone interested in design and fine craftsmanship. Throughout the five floors of this converted mansion the collection focuses on Spanish traditions, but places them in a wider context. The glassware from La Granja, for example, contrasts with centuries-old pieces dating from Greek and Roman times as well as more modern Lalique. Porcelain from Spanish factories compares with works from elsewhere in Europe, such as Meissen, Limoges and Sèvres.

The undoubted highlight is the famous tiled kitchen on the fourth floor, brought here from a palace in Valencia. Covered in hand-painted pictorial tiles, this is a snapshot of 18th-century life that shows the mistress of the house and her retinue of servants – from the butler in frock coat and buckled shoes to the African woman wielding a broom. Food historians note the copper pots, the leg of lamb, partridge, *chorizos* (sausages) and even a tray of cakes and *turrón* (nougat) that look good enough to eat. Most fun are the cats which are stealing a fish from the pan and an eel from the shopping basket.

Furniture, tapestries, an ornate silver tabletop showing all the signs of the zodiac – there is much to admire here. Don't, however, miss the room dedicated to the fan, that most Spanish of all fashion accessories. Follow its evolution from simple palm leaves to intricate designs in silk and mother-of-pearl. Even the language of the fan is deciphered.

http://mnartesdecorativas.mcu.es

🕂 20J ✉ Calle de Montalbán 12 ☎ 91 532 64 99 🕓 Tue–Sat 9:30–3, Sun, public hols 10–3 ✋ Inexpensive; free EU citizens under 18, over 65; free for all Sun Ⓜ Banco de España, Retiro

MUSEO NAVAL

You need a working knowledge of Spanish or naval history to get the best out of this small museum. In addition to numerous models of boats, there are vivid paintings depicting naval victories. A famous battle prize is the flag of the French battleship L' *Atlas* (Room VII). Napoleon presented ensigns to all his commanders before the Battle of Trafalgar in 1805 – this is the only one to survive. Don't miss Room XVII, where the routes of Spain's explorers are plotted on a world map covering an entire wall. Here, too, is the first map of the New World by a cartographer who had actually been there. Dated 1500, it was made by Juan de la Cosa, captain of the *Santa María*, one of the ships led by Columbus in 1492.

✚ 20J ✉ Paseo del Prado 5 ☎ 91 523 87 89 🕐 Tue–Sun 10–2. Closed Aug ✋ Free 🚇 Banco de España

MUSEO DEL PRADO

Best places to see, pages 44–45.

EXPLORING

PALACIO DE COMUNICACIONES

Nicknamed Nuestra Señora de las Comunicaciones, as if it were a cathedral, the Palacio de Comunicaciones dominates Plaza de la Cibeles (➤ 145). The Banco de Espana stands opposite; further south, on Paseo del Prado, is the Stock Exchange. These three grandiose buildings from the beginning of the 20th century were part of the city's earlier expansion programme.

However, the Spanish postal organization is moving out after a century of grandeur, and this historic landmark is once more in the spotlight. After an architectural facelift, it will become the City of Madrid's new municipal headquarters. One of the highlights will be an 'urban living room', a vast space open to the public under a

glass-roofed atrium. Glass elevators will whisk visitors up to the tower roof, where there will be a cafeteria and great views of the city, 60m (200ft) above street level. Arup and Arquimática, two architectural companies specializing in the renovation of historical buildings, are involved in what is expected to be yet another example of the 'new' Madrid – just as it was a century ago. A post office (open Mon–Sat), remains in operation (➤ 31).
www.correos.es

✚ 20J ✉ Plaza de la Cibeles s/n 🚇 Banco de España

PARQUE DEL RETIRO
Best places to see, pages 52–53.

EXPLORING

THE PASEOS

Madrid is split down the middle, from north to south, by a series of *paseos* or boulevards: the Paseo de la Castellana (4km/2.5 miles), the Paseo de Recoletos (1km/0.6 miles) and the Paseo del Prado (1.5km/1 mile, ➤ 122–123). These are interspersed by grand roundabouts, often graced by imposing statues and fountains, such as the Plaza de la Cibeles (➤ 145).

Most visitors enjoy the stretch of the Paseo del Prado linking the three great art museums: the Prado (➤ 44–45), the Museo

Nacional Centro de Arte Reina Sofía (➤ 42–43) and the Museo Thyssen-Bornemisza (➤ 48–49). Trees shade strollers along the eastern side of this *paseo*, which borders the Real Jardín Botánico (➤ 125).

The Paseo de Recoletos has echoes of Paris, with its glamorous cafés. The most famous is the Gran Café Gijón (➤ 59), known as a meeting place for writers and artists in the 1920s. Today, actors, agents and directors still meet to read scripts and clinch deals. In the evenings a pianist tinkles away.

The Paseo de la Castellana, which cuts through the modern part of the city, is lined with imposing office buildings and, to the north, the Estadio Santiago Bernabéu, home of Real Madrid football club (➤ 134). In summer, the Castellana is known for its *terrazas* (open-air cafés), which open late and close in the early hours. Locals have their favourite *terraza* where they meet to chat and drink, often to a background of music.

✚ 10A–20L

PUERTA DE ALCALÁ

Dominating the Plaza de Independencia, this handsome gate once straddled the main road to Alcalá de Henares (➤ 158–159). Another fine example of the work commissioned by Carlos III and designed by architect Francesco Sabatini, the gate dates back to 1778. Still visible are the scars from cannonballs fired in 1823, when a royalist army from France was sent to restore Ferdinand VII to the throne.

✚ 21H 🚇 Retiro ❓ Particularly attractive when illuminated at night

EXPLORING

a walk along the Paseo del Prado

Start at the Atocha Railway Station.

The 19th-century station has been converted into an astonishing botanic garden; the high-speed trains leave from the high-tech station annexe. Across the street is the Museo Nacional Centro de Arte Reina Sofía (➤ 42–43).

Walk north along the Paseo del Prado.

This is the southern end of a chain of boulevards passing several major attractions (➤ 120–121). Walk along the east side of the street, past the Real Jardín Botánico (➤ 125) and the Prado (➤ 44–45). On the left, in the Plaza de Cánovas del Castillo, is a fountain with a statue of Neptune. Beyond that is the Museo Thyssen-Bornemisza (➤ 48–49), the third of Madrid's spectacular art galleries.

Continue north on the Paseo del Prado.

Walk past the Hotel Ritz (Lealtad 5; ➤ 77), and the railings on the Plaza de la Lealtad, which

EASTERN MADRID

enclose an obelisk dedicated to the local heroes who died on 2 May 1808 in the revolt against the French. The next grand façade on the right (Lealtad 11) is the Bolsa, the Madrid Stock Exchange. Once past the Museo Naval (➤ 117), you reach the Plaza de la Cibeles (➤ 145), with its fountain. The grandiose building on the right is the Palacio de Comunicaciones (➤ 118–119), scheduled to be the new city hall. Off to the right, on the Calle de Alcalá, is the Puerta de Alcalá. This monumental arch, built by Carlos III, is considered the symbol of Madrid.

Distance 1.5km (1 mile)
Time One day, including visits
Start point Estación de Atocha ✚ 20L 🚇 Estación de Atocha
End point Plaza de la Cibeles ✚ 20H 🚇 Banco de España
Tea Hotel Ritz (€€) ✉ Plaza de la Lealtad 5 ☎ 91 701 67 67

EXPLORING

REAL FÁBRICA DE TAPICES

Not a museum, this factory hums with the sounds of men and women making and repairing carpets and tapestries. The methods have changed little, if at all, over the centuries since the van der Goten family was brought here from Flanders in the 18th century by Felipe V. The 200-year-old looms are still anchored by massive tree trunks to keep the tapestry taut, and woollen threads are still spun by hand, carefully mixed with silk to create some 3,000 subtly different shades.

Many of the tapestries are still based on cartoons (drawings) by the famous Spanish painters of the day, including Goya. The time and effort required to complete a tapestry is astonishing: 1sq m (10.75sq ft) takes four months and costs over

EASTERN MADRID

12,000. Visitors tend to 'ooh' and 'aah' as they stare at workers who are using medieval skills in a medieval setting.
www.realfabricadetapices.com
✚ 22M ✉ Calle de Fuenterrabía 2 ☎ 91 434 05 50
🕐 Mon–Fri 10–2. Closed Holy Week, Aug
✋ Inexpensive 🚇 Atocha RENFE, Menéndez Pelayo
❓ All visits in small guided groups every 45 mins

REAL JARDÍN BOTÁNICO

On a hot summer day there is nowhere better to stroll or snooze on a bench than these royal botanic gardens. In celebration of its bicentenary (1981), the geometric gardens were renovated and remodelled; today there are three terraced areas to explore. Closest to the Paseo del Prado are 16 plots devoted to plants and herbs used for cooking, medicines and decoration. Some are indigenous to Spain and Portugal. In the late afternoon, enjoy the heady scent of the aromatics in plot 11. Dotted with fountains, the middle terrace is a living encyclopaedia of plants – from the oldest

known to man to the most highly developed species – all arranged in the correct scientific order. Appropriately, a bust of Linnaeus, the Swedish botanist who invented this classification system for plants, overlooks the gardens. Like Kew Gardens in England, the Jardín Botánico is also a scientific institution, with a seed bank of plants from around the world as well as the Iberian Peninsula.
www.rjb.csic.es
✚ 20L ✉ Plaza de Murillo 2 ☎ 91 420 30 17 🕐 Daily 10–sunset. Closed 25 Dec, 1 Jan ✋ Inexpensive; over-65s and children under 10 free 🚇 Atocha

EXPLORING

HOTELS

AC Palacio del Retiro (€€€)
In a century-old building that was converted into a hotel in 2004, this beautiful hotel overlooks the Retiro and is close to the three major museums. By contrast, the elegant restaurant is contemporary in design and cuisine. Facilities include sauna, fitness centre and wi-fi.

✉ Alfonso XII 14 ☎ 91 523 74 60; www.hotelacpalaciodelretiro.com
Ⓜ Retiro

Agumar (€€)
Steps away from the Parque del Retiro, yet close to the Atocha railway station, this is really a four-star business hotel, but on weekends, the rates are attractive. Within walking distance of the three major art galleries. 245 standard, modern rooms.

✉ Paseo Reina Cristina 7 ☎ 91 552 69 00; www.hotelagumar.com
Ⓜ Atocha

Hospes Madrid (€€€)
A new boutique hotel (2007) with only 35 rooms, this five-star hotel overlooks the famous Plaza de la Independencia and the Puerta de Alcalá. Designed by architect José María de Aguilar, the original building dates from 1883. An exciting addition to Madrid's hip hotel scene.

✉ Plaza de la Independencia 3 ☎ 90 225 42 55; www.hospes.es Ⓜ Retiro, Banco de España

Hostal Castilla I (€)
Plain, simple and aimed at the budget-conscious, this renovated two-star hotel has 20 rooms close to Atocha station.

✉ Atocha 43, 2º D ☎ 91 532 57 38 Ⓜ Atocha

Hotel Ritz, Madrid (€€€)
Dating from 1910, this was the first grand, international hotel in Madrid. Five stars, 167 rooms, three restaurants, one in the flower-filled garden, and a fitness centre. Enjoy a luxurious, if expensive experience, near museums and Retiro Park (➤ 52–53).

EASTERN MADRID

✉ Plaza de la Lealtad 5 ☎ 91 701 67 67; www.ritzmadrid.com 🚇 Banco de España

NH Sur (€)
A useful, well-priced and practical hotel close to the Atocha railway station, the new Méndez Álvaro bus station, the three main art museums and the Parque del Retiro. All the usual requirements: air-conditioning, TV, wireless internet.
✉ Paseo Infanta Isabel 9 ☎ 91 539 94 00; www.nh-hoteles.es 🚇 Atocha

RESTAURANTS

El Prado (€–€€)
The museum has both a cafeteria (open Tue–Sun, 9–7:15) and a restaurant (open Tue–Sun 11:30–4).
✉ Paseo del Prado ☎ 91 330 29 00 🚇 Banco de España

Horcher (€€€)
Step back in time to old-fashioned luxury. Wild duck, venison and boar are the specialities in this German-influenced traditional haunt.
✉ Alfonso XII 6 ☎ 91 522 07 31 🕐 Lunch, dinner. Closed Sat lunch, Sun, public hols 🚇 Retiro

Restaurante Club 31 (€€)
Close to the Puerta de Alcalá, this is a refined international restaurant with splendid wines and classic dishes, from steak and salmon to chicken and excellent fish.
✉ Calle de Alcalá 58 ☎ 91 531 00 92 🕐 Lunch, dinner. Closed Aug 🚇 Banco de España

Viridiana (€€€)
Near the three famous art museums, this is imaginative modern Spanish cooking at its best, thanks to chef Abraham García. Perhaps the best wine list in Spain.
✉ Calle de Juan de Mena 14 ☎ 91 523 44 78 🕐 Lunch, dinner. Closed Sun 🚇 Banco de España, Retiro

SHOPPING

FASHION
MellyMello
Carolina Stephan set up her designer children's clothing company in 2004. Aimed at 2- to 12-year-olds, her collection uses only natural fibres, such as wool, alpaca, cotton and linen.
✉ Calle de Claudio Coello 97 ☎ 91 431 23 66; www.mellymello.com
Ⓜ Príncipe de Vergara

Van Cuatro
Stylish women's wear, with international designer labels.
✉ Calle de Narváez 26 ☎ 91 577 53 05 Ⓜ Goya, Príncipe de Vergara

GIFTS AND DESIGN
El Prado
A fine place to find quality souvenirs is in the museum's excellent Palacios y Museos shop. As well as fine reproductions of famous works, there are silk scarves and blouses, pictures and chocolates, ties and jewellery.
✉ Paseo del Prado ☎ 91 330 29 00 Ⓜ Banco de España

La Casa de los Chales
Spanish shawls, with their characteristic embroidery and fringe, come in all sorts of fabrics and a multitude of designs. Prices are just as broad ranging. Here, you can choose from wool as well as velvet and lace.
✉ Calle del Duque de Sesto 54 ☎ 91 574 25 73; www.lacasadeloschales.com Ⓜ Goya

Ordenatrium
An unusual shop that sells everything you need when you have to save space, from ingenious luggage and tie racks to shoe storage and hangers. Great fun, great imagination.
✉ Jorge Juan 69 ☎ 91 781 1142; www.ordenatrium.com Ⓜ Goya

NORTHERN MADRID

Northern Madrid

It is easy to fall into the trap of thinking that all of Madrid is medieval. But it is well worth getting out of the old heart. Salamanca, for example, is the elegant district to the northeast. Set out in a grid pattern, this is where the rich and famous live and where the shops are as grand as anywhere in the world. Directly north of the old city is Chueca, an area always associated with the gay community, but open to all, with fun bars and restaurants. Off to the west and northwest are more parks, as well as fine museums near the university district.

Further north, but easy to get to on the city's excellent Metro, is one of Madrid's most popular tourist attractions. Not a museum or a palace, it is the Santiago Bernabéu football stadium, home of CF Real Madrid, honoured by FIFA, the sport's world governing body, as the 'Best Club of the 20th Century'. Even if you cannot get a ticket to a match, it is worth doing the stadium tour. Nearby is Las Ventas, Madrid's bullring, regarded as the world's most prestigious arena for aficionados and matadors alike.

EXPLORING

CALLE DE SERRANO

Calle de Serrano is synonymous with 'expensive'. Like Fifth Avenue in New York or Bond Street in London, it is *the* place to go shopping for anything beautiful and costly. A broad thoroughfare, Calle de Serrano runs north–south through the elegant Salamanca district, which was laid out in a grid pattern in the late 19th century. Over the years, nearby streets have also sprouted fine shops. Stroll down Calle de Claudio Coello, parallel to Serrano, and explore cross streets such as Calle de Jorge Juan, Calle de Goya and Calle de José Ortega y Gasset, where limousines, their engines ticking over, wait outside designer boutiques.

11A–21H Serrano, Núñez de Balboa

NORTHERN MADRID

CASA DE AMÉRICA

In Spanish, the word 'América' tends to refer to Latin America rather than to the USA. Ties between Spain and her former colonies remain strong, and this lively cultural centre celebrates that connection. Since opening in 1992, it has hosted exhibitions, concerts, films and events reflecting Latin-American culture.

It is part of the elaborately decorated 19th-century Palacio de Linares. Supposedly haunted, it was the home of a wealthy financier whose son fell in love with a shop girl. Sent away to England, he returned to Madrid on his father's death. The couple married, but later discovered a letter explaining that the girl was the financier's illegitimate daughter. Pope León XIII told them that they could remain together but must be chaste. Their unhappy ghosts are said to inhabit the mansion.

www.casamerica.es

✚ 20H ✉ Paseo de Recoletos 2 ☎ 91 595 48 00 ⊕ Exhibitions: Mon–Sat 11–8, Sun, public hols 12–3 ✋ Free/inexpensive (exhibitions) 🍴 Snack bar, restaurant in Palacio (€–€€) Ⓜ Banco de España ❓ Shop sells Latin-American handicrafts

CENTRO CULTURAL CONDE DUQUE

It is worth checking the entertainment listings to see what is on at this handsome cultural centre. It was once the barracks for the royal bodyguard, and reflected the grandeur of Felipe V's Palacio Real to the south. Begun in 1720, it housed soldiers for 150 years.

Today, it is an important part of Madrid's cultural scene, holding special events and exhibitions throughout the year.

www.munimadrid.es

✚ 5E ✉ Calle de Conde Duque 11 ☎ 91 548 37 01 ⊕ Exhibitions: Thu–Sat 10–2, 6–9, Sun 11–2:30 ✋ Varies according to event Ⓜ Noviciado, San Bernardo, Ventura Rodríguez

ERMITA DE SAN ANTONIO DE LA FLORIDA

There are two small churches here, in this rather off-the-beaten-track location. The one on the left is a replica, built to hold services. On the right is the original *ermita* (hermitage), begun in 1792 by Charles IV's Italian architect, Francisco Fontana, on the site of a previous hermitage, and now a museum dedicated to Goya, one of Spain's greatest artists. The ceiling he painted, revolutionary in technique and subject matter, was a turning point in the history of art.

Goya was 52 when he began this project in 1798. He had just recovered from a severe illness that left him deaf, but worked from August to mid-December, using brushes, sponges and even his thumbs to portray St Anthony raising a murdered man from the dead. Use the handy mirrors to study the characters: St Anthony, the victim and the man falsely accused of the crime – the saint's own father. This is not an idealized scene with important nobles and ecclesiastics; these are real people showing real emotions, wearing ordinary clothes. It's easy to imagine how this painting shocked the establishment at the time.

A 200-year-old custom centres on St Anthony, 'the matchmaker'. His feast day on 13 June draws unmarried women to the Ermita for an unusual ritual. Standing before the baptismal font, each woman drops 13 pins into it, presses her palm down into the water and then lifts it out. The number of pins sticking to the skin of her hand indicates the number of suitors she will have that year.

www.munimadrid.es/ermita

✠ 2F ✉ Glorieta de San Antonio de la Florida 5 ☎ 91 542 07 22
🕒 Tue–Fri 9:30–8, Sat, Sun 10–2. Closed public hols ✋ Free
🍴 Casa Mingo (next door) (€) Ⓜ Príncipe Pío

NORTHERN MADRID

EXPLORING

ESTADIO SANTIAGO BERNABÉU
Madrid may be crowded with churches, but the most popular modern shrine is this football stadium – the home of Real Madrid. Set on a broad boulevard, with its own Metro station, the 80,000-seat stadium hosted the 1982 World Cup Final. Founded in 1902, 'Real' became one of the most famous football clubs in the world. The name means Royal, and the club has proved to be a majestic force in football, so much so that in 1998, FIFA, the world governing body, awarded them the accolade, 'the best club in the history of football'.

Even if you can't get to a game, you can experience the atmosphere by visiting the Sala de Trofeos (trophy room) or, even better, by joining a guided tour. Visitors are shown a panoramic view of the inside of the stadium, the pitch (field) and players' tunnel, the away dressing room and trophy room. Crammed with dazzling silver trophies and resonating with screams of '*Gol!, Gol!, Gol!*' this is a football fan's paradise. Numerous video screens show clips from great matches of the past, including their nine European Cup triumphs between 1956 and 2006, as well as 17 Spanish Cups and 30 Spanish league championships.

Real participates in many sports. Their basketball team, for example, has an equally glowing history, having won eight European Cups plus the 1981 world club title.

www.realmadrid.com

🎫 10A (off map) ✉ Calle Concha Espina ☎ 91 398 43 00 (stadium), 902 324 324 (tickets) 🕐 Sala de Trofeos: Tue–Sun 10:30–7:30. Closed 3 hours before a match. Museum (gate 5) open Tue–Sun 10:30–7:30. Guided tour from Gate 7 Mon–Sat 10–7, Sun, public hols 10:30–6:30; no tours from 5 hours before a match ✋ Sala de Trofeos: inexpensive. Museum: expensive Ⓜ Santiago Bernabéu 🚌 14, 27, 40, 43, 120, 147, 150

IGLESIA DE SANTA BÁRBARA
Known to locals as the Iglesia de las Salesas, this massive baroque church is one of the most impressive in the city. The

NORTHERN MADRID

monastery of the Royal Salesian Order was founded by Barbara of Braganza, the Portuguese wife of Fernando VI, as a spiritual refuge from her domineering mother-in-law, in case the king died before her (as it turned out he outlived her). The church of Santa Bárbara was designed by the French architect, Françoise Carlier, in 1749 and completed nine years later. Pause to admire the elaborately sculpted façade before going inside. Here the highlights are Francesco de Mura's *Visitation* over the high altar, paintings by Corrado Giaquinto, responsible for the frescoes in the Palacio Real, and the tombs of Fernando and his wife by Francisco Gutiérrez.

🕂 19G ✉ Calle del General Castaños 2 ☎ 91 319 48 11 🕙 Daily 5–7 and during Mass 🖐 Free 🚇 Colón, Alonso Martínez

EXPLORING

MUSEO DE AMÉRICA
Best places to see, pages 38–39.

MUSEO ARQUEOLÓGICO NACIONAL
The National Archaeological Museum's collection reflects Mediterranean cultures as well as those of the Iberian peninsula. Although the old-fashioned, glass-cased displays could put off the younger generation, exhibits such as the *Dama de Elche* are fascinating. Discovered near Alicante, this finely-carved bust of a noblewoman from Elche dates from around the 4th century BC; the

NORTHERN MADRID

hole at the back probably held the ashes of a well-born person. Like a photograph in *Vogue* magazine, her elaborate headdress and jewellery reflect the fashions of Iberia, but they also relate to Greek and Celtic styles. Moreover, they can be traced through the centuries to the traditional hairstyles of Valencia. Other treasures in the museum include porcelain from the Buen Retiro factory, Greek pottery, and an intriguing Roman sundial. In the garden, a specially dug-out underground room contains reproductions of the famous prehistoric cave paintings of bison and deer from Altamira. Explanations in several languages are available.

www.man.es
🕂 20G ✉ Calle del Serrano 13 ☎ 91 577 79 12/91 577 79 19/20 🕓 Tue–Sat 9:30–8, Sun, public hols 9:30–2 ✋ Inexpensive; free for EU citizens under 18, over-65, free to all Sat pm, Sun 🚇 Serrano, Colón, Retiro

MUSEO CERRALBO

The 17th Marquis of Cerralbo (1845–1922) was passionate about politics and the arts. His collection, which has to be shown as he left it, includes 50,000 'works of art, archaeological objects and curios', gathered from around the world. Although the best-known of his paintings is *The Ecstasy of St Francis of Assisi* by El Greco, there is also porcelain, Greek and Roman pottery, furniture, swords and oriental armour. Connoisseurs appreciate the aristocratic mansion as much as the artefacts. The sumptuous ballroom (renovated in 1999) contrasts with the practical office-library; even the parquet floors in the dining room and billiard room demand admiration.

http://museocerralbo.mcu.es
🕂 15G ✉ Calle Ventura Rodríguez 17 ☎ 91 547 36 46 🕓 Tue–Sat 9:30–3, Sun 10–3; Jul, Aug Tue–Sat 9:30–2, Sun, public hols 10–2 ✋ Inexpensive, free under 18, over-65; free to all Wed, Sun, 8 Jul 🚇 Plaza de España, Ventura Rodríguez

EXPLORING

MUSEO CHICOTE
Not a museum, but a cocktail bar! Founded in 1931 by Perico Chicote to 'mix drinks, lives and opinions', this art deco bar survives more on memories than present-day glamour. Photos of Frank Sinatra, Salvador Dalí, Bette Davis and Ernest Hemingway line the walls, but as to who sat where and when, that depends on which waiter you ask. Chicote's museum of odd drinks and bottles has gone, but *madrileños* still come late for a cocktail, and on weekends it's the busiest museum in town – after midnight that is.

www.museo-chicote.com

✚ 18H ✉ Gran Vía 12 ☎ 91 532 67 37 🕐 Mon–Sat 4pm–4am
Ⓜ Gran Vía, Banco de Espana

MUSEO DE ESCULTURA AL AIRE LIBRE
Every day, office workers pass a dozen or so works by some of Spain's foremost 20th-century sculptors, such as Eduardo Chillida, Joan Miró and Julio González. At this unusual open-air sculpture gallery, the pieces, some of them massive, shelter beneath the 1970 road bridge that crosses the Paseo de la Castellana at Calle de Juan Bravo. Chillida's massive concrete *La Sirena Varada* is suspended on cables; Miró's *Mère Ubu* is a delightful bronze figure; and *La pequeña hoz (The little sickle)* is a striking creation by González. The exhibition is always free and always open.

www.munimadrid.es/museoairelibre

✚ 11D ✉ Paseo de la Castellana 41 ♿ Free Ⓜ Rubén Darío 🚌 5, 7, 9, 14, 19, 27, 45, 147, 150

MUSEO LÁZARO GALDIANO
Best places to see, pages 40–41.

NORTHERN MADRID

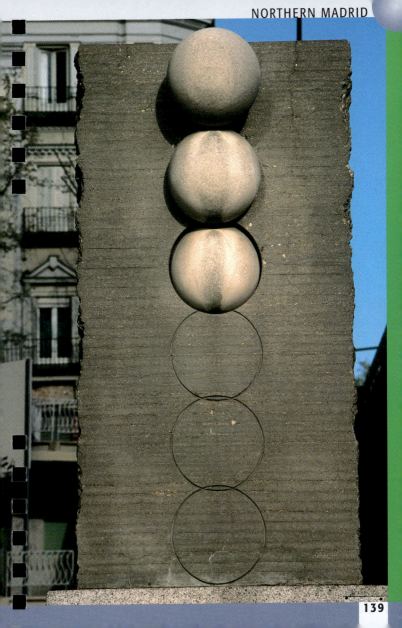

EXPLORING

MUSEO ROMÁNTICO

The Marqués de la Vega-Inclán (1858–1942) set up the country's tourist infrastructure and initiated the *paradores*, the national group of hotels in former castles and monasteries. His collection of 19th-century paintings, books and furniture formed the nucleus of this somewhat eccentric but entertaining museum of period ephemera (fans, old photo albums, cigar cases, duelling pistols, paintings etc), dedicated to artists and writers of a romantic bent.

NORTHERN MADRID

✝ 8E ✉ Calle de San Mateo 13 ☎ 91 448 10 45 and 91 448 01 63
Ⓜ Tribunal, Alonso Martínez

MUSEO SOROLLA
Best places to see, pages 46–47.

MUSEO DEL TRAJE
Opened in 2004, the Museum of Costume has been a huge success. The colourful collection, which includes everything from shoes to mantillas, draws on more then 21,000 items. Walk through the galleries and you can trace the evolution of Spanish clothing and fashions from medieval times to the 20th century. Included are designs by the great Spanish 20th-century couturiers, Mariano Fortuny, born in Granada, and Cristobal Balenciaga, a Basque who went on to take the Parisian fashion world by storm. The prize exhibit is the 13th-century trousseau of the Infanta María, daughter of Ferdinand III. But a favourite with visitors is the display of women's underwear, from the bodices of the 17th century to the girdles of the 1940s.

Set in a quiet garden, the building itself is stunning, with a café, the posh Bokado restaurant and a terrace for outdoor dining in summer.

www.museodeltraje.mcu.es
✝ 1B ✉ Avenida Juan de Herrera 2 ☎ 91 550 47 00 🕐 Tue–Sat 9:30–7, Sun, public hols 10–3. Jul, Aug Thu 9:30am–10:30pm 💰 Inexpensive; free under 18, oveer 65 Ⓜ Moncloa, Ciudad Universitaria ❓ Audio-guides in Spanish, English, French. Museum café and restaurant

141

EXPLORING

a walk along the Gran Vía

Start in the Plaza de España.

The focal point of this large square is the memorial to Miguel Cervantes. A statue of the author, book in hand, looks over his famous characters – Don Quixote and

Sancho Panza. The two tallest structures, the Edificio España and the Torre de Madrid, were designed and built by the prolific Otamendi brothers in the early 1950s.

Walk southeast down the Gran Vía.

When Madrid expanded in the early 1900s, over 300 houses and 14 ancient streets were demolished to make way for this boulevard. New buildings, some inspired by the North American skyscraper, include 1920s–30s cinemas, such as the Capitol in the Carrión building (Gran Vía 41) and the Cine Callao (Plaza del Callao 3). The Palacio de la Prensa (Plaza del Callao 4) originally provided office workers with everything from entertainment to shops and restaurants, all under one roof.

Continue east along the Gran Vía.

At Gran Vía 28 is the Telefónica (➤ 148). This American-designed skyscraper (1929) was the tallest in the city for some 25 years. From here on, buildings are older and more heavily decorated. Note the extravagant roof-top

NORTHERN MADRID

embellishments of the 1913 Edificio del Banco Central (Gran Vía 18) and the Edificio la Estrella (Gran Vía 7 and 10). Number 7 shows a Moorish influence. The walk ends at the Parisian-style Edificio Metrópolis, which is crowned by a statue of Winged Victory.

Distance 1.3km (0.8 miles)
Time 3 hours including visits
Start point Plaza de España ✚ 15G Ⓜ Plaza de España
End point Corner of Gran Vía and Calle de Alcalá ✚ 19H Ⓜ Banco de España
Lunch Museo del Jamón (€) ✉ Gran Vía 72 ☎ 91 541 20 23

EXPLORING

NORTHERN MADRID

PLAZA DE LA CIBELES

There are three spots dear to the hearts of *madrileños*: the Puerta de Alcalá arch; the statue of the bear and the *madroño* (madrona tree) in Puerto del Sol (▶ 100–101); and the Cibeles fountain in the roundabout that links the Paseo del Prado and the Paseo de Recoletos. Cybeles, the Greek goddess of fertility, sits in her chariot, which is drawn by two magnificent lions. The fountain itself was designed for Carlos III by Ventura Rodríguez in the 18th century, but these details are of little interest to Real Madrid football fans. They come here to celebrate their victories. Fans from rival Atlético de Madrid congregate at the next fountain to the south, with its statue of Neptune.
✚ 20H

PLAZA DE COLÓN

This rather stark open square gets its name from Cristóbal Colón (Christopher Columbus), who discovered the Americas. The explorer stands on top of an elegant 17m-tall (56ft) column, erected in 1893, just after the 400th anniversary celebrations of the 1492 voyage. Beneath the square is the Centro Cultural de la Villa de Madrid (Cultural Centre). At the eastern end of the plaza, next to Calle Serrano, in what is called the Jardínes de Descubrimiento (Discovery Gardens), is the Monumento al Descubrimiento de América, a massive concrete wall sculpture by Joaquín Vaquero Turcios (1977).
✚ 10F

EXPLORING

PLAZA DE TOROS DE LAS VENTAS

Whether you are for or against bullfighting, Las Ventas is an astonishing building. Dating from 1929, this is the most prestigious arena in the world – a 22,000-seat cathedral of bullfighting. A classic example of Moorish-inspired architecture, with pink brick and decorative tilework, it towers above the Las Ventas Metro stop. In the spacious forecourt, lifesize statues make convenient meeting places for friends before a *corrida* (fight). Poised in mid-air to the left of the main entrance is '*El Yiyo*' (José Cubero), while the legendary Antonio Bienvenida is carried shoulder high by admirers (to the right of the main entrance). Off to one side, a *torero* doffs his cap to Dr Fleming, the inventor of penicillin, which has saved the lives of many bullfighters. Along a wall facing the southwest side of the stadium is a mural of nine lifesize bulls and their keepers.

Fights are usually at 7 in the evening, and are said to be the only events in Spain that start right on time. Crowds gather early looking for tickets and buying nuts and sweets from stalls. The most prestigious *corridas* are during the *feria* of San Isidro, the month-long festival in May, when some 30 take place.

On the north side of the arena is the **Museo Taurino.** This small museum is a Hall of Fame for bullfighting. It traces the development of the modern style and honours the legends of the ring, who are all known by their nicknames. Portraits and busts include stars of the 19th century: 'Cúchares' (Francisco Arjona), celebrated for his innovative movements, and the rivals 'Lagartijo' (Rafael Molina)

NORTHERN MADRID

and 'Frascuelo' (Salvador Sánchez). Although words such as 'artistic' and 'elegant' describe their skills, the litany of deaths from wounds and infections is sobering. The famous 'Manolete', for example, died after being gored on 28 August 1947. The white-and-gold costume he wore that day, plus his pink cape embroidered with roses and violets, is on display next to the blood transfusion machine that failed to save his life. Credit is also given to the supporting *picadores* and *banderilleros* and even famous bulls: the head of the bull that killed Manuel García Espartero (1865–94) is proudly displayed.

www.taquillatoros.com

✚ 24G (off map) ✉ Calle de Alcalá 237 ☎ 91 356 22 00 (stadium), 91 725 18 57 (museum)
🕓 Bullfights: Mar–Oct; Museum: Tue–Fri 9:30–2:30, Sun, public hols 10–1; Nov–Feb Mon–Fri 9:30–2:30. 30-min tour of bullring Tue–Sun 10–2 (English spoken)
✋ Bullfights inexpensive–expensive; museum free; tour moderate 🚇 Las Ventas

TELEFÉRICO

The most spectacular views of the Madrid skyline are from the Teleférico cable-car. Since 1969 it has glided from the Paseo del Pintor Rosales, just north of the Plaza de España, across to the scrubby parkland of the Casa de Campo. On board, a taped, but muffled, Spanish commentary points out landmarks as you swing across the gardens of the Parque del Oeste, the twin domes of the Ermita de San Antonio de la Florida (➤ 132) and the Río Manzanares. The 11-minute, 2.5km (1.5-mile) ride terminates in a modern building with a very ordinary cafeteria and snack bar.
www.teleferico.com/madrid

🞣 2E ✉ Paseo del Pintor Rosales s/n ☎ 91 541 11 18 🕑 Daily noon–sunset in summer; Sep–Mar mainly weekends, public hols
💰 Inexpensive 🍴 Restaurant/café (€) 🚇 Argüelles

TELEFÓNICA

One of the city's first skyscrapers, the Telefónica opened in 1929 as the headquarters of Spain's national telephone service, symbolizing the country's move into the modern era. Take time to see the rotating exhibitions drawn from the telephone company's collection of paintings and sculptures by Spanish artists such as Picasso, Chillida, Gris and Tapiès.

🞣 18H ✉ Fuencarral 3 ☎ 91 522 66 45 (gallery) 🕑 Tue–Fri 10–2, 5–8; Sat 11–8, Sun, public hols 11–2 💰 Free with passport 🚇 Gran Vía

NORTHERN MADRID

HOTELS

Apartohotel Eraso (€)
This 3-star hotel in the Salamanca district is good value for families and has 31 modern rooms. Own garage.
✉ Calle de Ardemans 13 ☎ 91 355 32 00; www.aphotel-eraso.com
🚇 Diego de León

Hotel AC Monte Real (€€–€€€)
On the northwest edge of Madrid, near the Puerta de Hierro golf course and the motorway. With 72 luxury rooms, this quiet 5-star hotel is ideal for business meetings.
✉ Calle del Aroyofresno 17 ☎ 91 736 52 73; www.ac-hoteles.com

Hotel Alcalá (€€–€€€)
This 146-room hotel has surprisingly stylish rooms with lots of polished wood. Helpful staff.
✉ Calle de Alcalá 66 ☎ 91 435 10 60; www.nh-hotels.com 🚇 Príncipe de Vergara

Hostal Breogan y Kryse (€)
Handy for sightseeing and shopping, these two-*hostals*-in-one offer good value. Rooms are clean, reasonably sized and have ensuite bathroom, TV and ceiling fan.
✉ Calle Fuencarral 25 1° ☎ 91 531 1512 🚇 Gran Via

Hotel Husa Moncloa (€€)
A modern 4-star hotel, popular with businesspeople during the week and overseas holidaymakers on weekends.
✉ Calle Serrano Jover 1 ☎ 91 542 45 82; www.husamoncloa.com
🚇 Argüelles, Ventura Rodríguez

Hotel Lagasca (€€€)
A 3-star hotel near the shops of the Serrano and surrounded by good restaurants. Opened in the early 1990s, its 100 rooms are plain, in minimalist style; striking bathrooms.
✉ Calle de Lagasca 64 ☎ 91 575 46 06; www.nh-hotels.com 🚇 Velázquez, Serrano

Hotel Orense (€€)
Just off the Paseo de la Castillana, this 140-room, 4-star hotel is also ideal for the business district.

✉ Calle de Pedro Teixeira 5 ☎ 91 597 15 68; www.rafaelhoteles.com
🚇 Estadio Bernabéu

RESTAURANTS

Angel (€)
See page 58.

La Barraca (€€€)
This is the place for authentic paella and other rice-based specialities from the Valencian region.

✉ Calle de la Reina 29 ☎ 91 532 71 54 🕐 Lunch, dinner 🚇 Banco de España

Brasserie de Lista (€–€€)
See page 58.

Divina La Cocina (€€)
Marinated tuna is the speciality of this stylish, highly innovative establishment in the heart of the Chueca district. The Spanish fusion dishes on the set menu are excellent value. Book ahead.

✉ Colmenares 13 ☎ 91 531 37 65 🕐 Lunch, dinner 🚇 Chueca

La Trainera (€€–€€€)
A plain restaurant in the expensive Serrano district, this is one of the best places for fish in Madrid. Try oysters, crabs, *gambas* (prawns), *sopa de mariscos* (fish soup).

✉ Calle Lagasca 60 ☎ 91 576 80 35 🕐 Lunch, dinner. Closed Sun, Aug
🚇 Serrano

Zalacaín (€€€)
One of Madrid's top restaurants, with an international menu and Basque specialities. Advance booking essential.

✉ Calle de Alvarez de Baena 4 ☎ 91 561 59 35 🕐 Lunch, dinner. Closed Sat lunch, Sun, Aug, Easter 🚇 Gregorio Marañón

NORTHERN MADRID

SHOPPING

ANTIQUES AND BOOKS
La Casa del Libro
The largest bookstore in Spain. As well as thousands of Spanish titles, there is a useful corner selling books and guides in several foreign languages. One of five branches in Madrid.
✉ Gran Vía 29 ☎ 90 202 64 02 🚇 Gran Vía

Casa Postal
This old-fashioned shop is a rummager's delight, crammed with old and antique postcards, as well as maps, photographs and 'curiosities', such as train sets and unused calendars from 1949.
✉ ☎ alle de la Libertad 37 ☎ 91 532 70 37 🚇 Chueca

ARTS, CRAFTS, GIFTS AND DESIGN
Antigua Casa Crespo
This old-fashioned shop is known for selling alpargatas, espadrilles, or rope-soled shoes, that come in all shapes and sizes.
✉ Calle del Divino Pastor 29 ☎ 91 521 56 54 🚇 San Bernardo, Bilbao

Expresión Negra
A fascinating emporium dealing in everything associated with African arts and crafts. You can pick up items like patchwork quilts, briefcases, woven baskets, rugs and much more besides.
✉ Calle Piamonte 15 ☎ 91 319 95 27 🚇 Chueca, Colón

Gion
In trendy Chueca, the speciality here is exquisite embroidered silk kimonos, surrounded by handicrafts from the Kyoto region of Japan, from where the owner hails.
✉ Calle de Augusto Figueroa 27 ☎ 91 523 97 26 🚇 Chueca

Popland
You could spend hours here, window shopping the crazy miscellany of 1950s and '60s popular kitsch – everything from Judy Garland cut-out dolls to James Bond posters and Beatles figurines.
✉ Calle Manuela Malasaña 24 ☎ 91 591 21 20 🚇 Tribunal

Santa

This store sells over 60 varieties of chocolate, including pralines, truffles and *marron glacés* (candied chestnuts). The speciality is *leña vieja* (chocolates shaped like logs and sold at Christmas).
✉ Calle de Serrano 56 ☎ 91 576 86 46 🚇 Serrano

FASHION
Adolfo Domínguez

Adolfo Domínguez has 12 fashion and accessory shops, including several in the Serrano shopping area.
✉ Calle de Serrano 18 ☎ 91 577 82 80 🚇 Serrano

Homeless

This elegant boutique started out in 1994 raising money for the homeless of San Sebastian. It now has its own label offering casual clothing mainly to young professionals.
✉ Calle Fuencarral 16 ☎ 91 524 17 28 🚇 Gran Via

Jésus del Pozo

Features one of Spain's leading and most famous young designers.
✉ Calle del Almirante 9 ☎ 91 531 36 46 🚇 Colón, Chueca

Mango

Mainly for the young and young-at-heart, who recognize good value when they see it.
✉ Calle de Goya 83 ☎ 91 435 39 58 🚇 Goya

Purification Garcia

The famous Spanish designer's Salamanca store showcases an alluring range of ready-made men's and women's clothing.
✉ Calle Serrano 28 and 92 ☎ 91 435 80 13/91 576 72 76 🚇 Serrano, Nuñez de Balboa

Roberto Verino

This Spanish designer has several stores in central Madrid, with clothes and accessories for men and women.
✉ Calle de Claudio Coello 27 ☎ 91 577 73 81 🚇 Serrano

NORTHERN MADRID

Zara
Up-to-the-minute styles at low prices have made this chain of stores a success not just in Spain but internationally as well. This is one of the largest branches in Madrid.
✉ Gran Vía 32 ☎ 91 521 12 83 Ⓜ Gran Vía

FOOD AND DRINK
Horno San Onofre
Sample the regional variety of Spanish cakes and tarts, as well as seasonal ones, traditionally made to celebrate saints' feast days. The speciality is the sponge cake-like *tarta de Santiago*.
✉ Calle de San Onofre 3 ☎ 91 532 90 60 Ⓜ Gran Vía

Museo del Jamón
This restaurant-shop is one of a chain that is hung with haunches of ham. The choice is enormous.
✉ Gran Vía 72 ☎ 91 541 20 23 Ⓜ Plaza de Espana, Santo Domingo

Patrimonio Comunal Olivarero
In a country where olive oil is used in virtually every dish, it is not surprising to find a shop that sells nothing but *aceite de oliva virgen extra*, the best olive oil you can get.
✉ Calle de Mejía Lequerica 1 ☎ 91 308 05 05 Ⓜ Alonso Martínez, Tribunal

Reserva y Cata
This basement wine merchant in Chueca can easily be overlooked, but its selection of Spanish wines and liquers is among the best in the city.
✉ Calle de Conde de Xiquena 13 ☎ 91 319 04 01 Ⓜ Colon, Banco de España

LEATHER GOODS
Camper
Cheerful and comfortable, Camper's designs have influenced shoe trends for over a decade.
✉ Calle de Ayala 13 ☎ 91 431 43 45 Ⓜ Serrano

EXPLORING

Las Bailarinas
Brightly painted shoes with original designs from Monica García are the speciality of this Chueca store which also sells bags and other fashion accessories.
✉ Calle Piamonte 19 ☎ 91 319 90 69 🚇 Chueca

Loewe
Enrique Loewe started a leather goods shop in Calle Echegaray back in 1846 and it is still world-famous for its quality.
✉ Calle de Serrano 26 and 34 ☎ 91 577 60 56 🚇 Serrano

ENTERTAINMENT

BARS, CLUBS AND LIVE MUSIC

Chesterfield Café
Opened in 1997, the theme here, like the name, is American, with American bands and American beer.
✉ Calle de Serrano Jover 5 ☎ 91 542 28 17 🕐 1:30pm–2am. Closed Sun 🚇 Argüelles

Clamores
Although the speciality is jazz, you can expect almost any act to turn up here, including reggae, blues and Latin American folk.
✉ Calle de Alburquerque 14 ☎ 91 445 79 38 🕐 6pm–3am; Fri, Sat until 4am. Shows start at 10:30pm 🚇 Bilbao

Fortuny
The Fortuny is one of the celebrity sanctuaries of Madrid, however, there is a very strict dress code at this glitzy nightclub.
✉ Calle de Fortuny 34 ☎ 91 319 05 88 🕐 2pm–dawn. Closed Sat, Sun lunch 🚇 Rubén Darío

Garamond
A *discoteca* with a difference, in the elegant Salamanca district, with medieval arches, painted ceilings, stones walls and suits of armour. There are even magicians and jugglers. Expensive and difficult to get into.
✉ Calle Claudio Coello 10 ☎ 91 576 84 02 🕐 10pm–5:30am 🚇 Colón

NORTHERN MADRID

Houdini Club de Magia
The Spanish still enjoy a good, old-fashioned magician. This club also has a rather spooky atmosphere.
✉ Calle de Garcia Luna 13 ☎ 91 416 42 74 🕒 8:30pm–2am. Closed Sun, Mon Ⓜ Cruz del Rayo

Moby Dick
Hugely popular, hot and sweaty, this club has a varied schedule of live music and DJs throughout the week.
✉ Avenida de Brasil 5 ☎ 91 555 76 71 🕒 9:30pm–6am. Closed Sun Ⓜ Santiago Bernabéu

THEATRE, MUSIC AND DANCE
Casa de América
This cultural centre dedicated to things Latin American (➤ 131) has presentations of film, plays and music.
✉ Paseo de Recoletos 2 ☎ 91 595 48 00; www.casamerica.es 🕒 Times vary, check listings Ⓜ Banco de España

Centro Cultural Conde Duque
This cultural centre (➤ 131 has a busy schedule year round, but it is at its best in the summer (mid-Jun to mid-Sep) when the courtyard is taken over by the Veranos de la Villa, a summer festival of jazz, classical music, ballet and opera. Several other sites in the city also take part in this festival.
✉ Calle de Conde Duque 11 ☎ 91 588 58 34 🕒 Box office: 10:30–2, 5:30–9. Closed Mon Ⓜ Ventura Rodríguez, Noviciado, San Bernardo

Centro Cultural de la Villa
There are plans to rebuild this modern cultural centre, currently situated underground, behind the waterfall of the Plaza Colón. As the city's official cultural centre, it stages a wide variety of performances year round, but is particularly known for *zarzuela* (light opera) and dance.
✉ Plaza de Colón ☎ 91 480 03 00 🕒 Box office: Mon–Fri 9:30–2:30, 5–7. Closed Mon Ⓜ Colón

Excursions

Alcalá de Henares	158–159
Aranjuez	160–161
A drive south of Madrid	162–163
El Escorial	164–165
Manzanares El Real	166–167
El Pardo	167
A drive around the Guadarrama Mountains	168–169
Segovia	170–171
A drive to Segovia and the mountains	172–173
Toledo	174–175
A walk around Toledo	176–177

EXCURSIONS

ALCALÁ DE HENARES

In 1998, UNESCO recognized Alcalá de Henares as the first town designed and built exclusively as a university town. About 30km (18 miles) due east of Madrid, the Universidad Complutense was founded in 1498, and was soon one of Europe's great seats of learning. In the past 25 years, the area around the Plaza de Cervantes, the heart of the old town, has been successfully restored. What were *colegios* (or student halls of residence) have been converted into schools, hotels and restaurants, but the

EXCURSIONS

ornate Renaissance façade of the **Colegio Mayor de San Ildefonso** (University of Alcalá de Henares) gives some idea of the original grandeur of the university headquarters. This administered 40 colleges and 10,000 students. Inside were three *patios* or courtyards. The third, El Trilingüe (1557), was where students from the schools of Hebrew, Greek and Latin would meet to chat in three languages. The Paraninfo (Great Hall) is still used for solemn university ceremonies, while the 15th-century chapel of San Ildefonso holds a richly sculpted marble memorial to the hugely influential Catholic leader, Cardinal Cisneros, the founder of the university.

Alcalá de Henares was also the birthplace of Miguel de Cervantes Saavedra (1547–1616), author of the international favourite, *El Quijote* (or *Don Quixote*). At No 48 on the attractive Calle Mayor main street is the **Casa Natal de Cervantes.** This is a reproduction of the writer's alleged birthplace, with an interior *patio* typical of the 16th century, and appropriate furniture for the era. Be sure to take home the local delicacy: *almendras garrapiñadas* (caramel covered almonds).

🚆 Cervantes Train: weekends mid-Apr to Jun, Sep–1st week Dec, leaves Atocha Madrid 11am, departs Alcalá 7pm

ℹ️ Plaza de Cervantes ☎ 91 889 26 94 🕐 Daily 10–2, 5–7:30. Closed Mon Jul, Aug. Plaza de los Santos Niños ☎ 91 881 06 34 🕐 Hours as above, but closed Tue Jul, Aug

Colegio Mayor de San Ildefonso

✉ Plaza de San Diego ☎ 91 885 40 17 🕐 Mon–Fri guided tours 11, 12, 1, 5, 6, 7; Sat, Sun, public hols on the half hour from 11–2, 5–7:30 💰 Inexpensive

Casa Natal de Cervantes

✉ Calle Mayor 48 ☎ 91 889 96 54; www.museo-casa-natal-cervantes.org
🕐 Tue–Sun 10–6 💰 Free

EXCURSIONS

ARANJUEZ

Thanks to the haunting theme of the *Concierto de Aranjuez* by Joaquín Rodrigo, music-lovers around the world know the name of this town. Just 50km (31 miles) south of Madrid, Aranjuez became a royal retreat 300 years ago. Today it is a popular destination for *madrileños*, who come for a day out, particularly in early summer when the asparagus and *fresones* (local strawberries) are in season. They stroll along tree-lined boulevards and through the gardens, take a boat ride on the Río Tajo (River Tagus) and tour the **Palacio Real.** This enormous baroque palace was built in the early 18th century for Felipe V. Although the façade and the interior remain much as they were, two wings were added later. Inside are paintings and frescoes and, best of all, the Sala de las Porcelanas. The porcelain tiles, made in Madrid, portray scenes from Chinese life, as well as children's games.

Heading east from the palace, follow the Calle de la Reina to the Jardín del Príncipe and, further along, the **Casa del Labrador.** Named the Worker's Cottage, it is opulently decorated and full of treasures, such as the Gabinete de Platino, with dazzling inlays of platinum, gold and bronze. Aranjuez is at its loveliest in March and April when the gardens are in bloom, but is most fun in May during the festivities for San Fernando (30 May) and in September, during the Fiestas del Motín. On weekends between April and June take the *Tren de la Fresa* (Strawberry Train) with its wooden carriages, steam engine and costumed hostesses distributing strawberries.

www.aranjuez.es

🚌 *Tren de la Fresa*, Atocha, Madrid weekends, public hols Apr–Jun ☎ 90 224 02 02 💰 Expensive ❓ 35-min tour on tourist trolley. Hourly from tourist office ☎ 92 514 22 74

EXCURSIONS

🛈 Plaza de San Antonio ☎ 91 891 04 27 🕐 Tue–Sun 10–2, 4–6 (summer); 10–1, 3–5 (winter)

Palacio Real, Casa del Labrador
☎ 91 891 07 40 ☎ 91 891 07 40 🕐 Apr–Sep Tue–Sun 10–6:15; Oct–Mar 10–5:15 ✋ Inexpensive, Wed free for EU citizens

EXCURSIONS

a drive south of Madrid

This route south includes three historic towns: one ancient, one royal and one a fortress.

Leave Madrid on the E-901, then take the A-3 for Chinchón. Before the main exit to Arganda, take the turning for Chinchón, the M-311. Take the left turn for Morata de Tajuña, with its view over the valley. Once on flat ground, you pass Anís de Chinchón, the distillery of the popular aniseed-flavoured drink. Then it's up to the opposite ridge, and down into the next valley, where Chinchón stands high on a hillside.

Head for the Plaza Mayor, a perfect film set for a costume drama in medieval Spain. Surrounded by rows of balconied houses, it is a ready-made arena, where bullfights and

EXCURSIONS

theatrical performances are still held. Have lunch at one of the many restaurants with tables outdoors. A former convent has been converted into a stylish *parador* (government-run country hotel). Parking is difficult in town, so leave the car on the outskirts and walk into the centre.

From Chinchón, take the M-305 for Aranjuez.

Villaconejos, known for its melons, is a typical blend of old and new, the attractive and bland. Continue to Aranjuez (➤ 160–161).

From Aranjuez, take the N-400 for Ocaña and Toledo.

You can see Toledo's castle from afar, standing guard over the plain below. Park in one of the car parks at the foot of the hill and explore this walled city on foot (➤ 176–177).

Return to Madrid on the N-401 motorway.

Distance 200km (124 miles)
Time 9 hours with stops, 5 hours without stops
Start/end point Madrid
Lunch La Perdiz (€–€€) ✉ Calle de los Reyes Católicos 7, Toledo
☎ 925 21 46 58

EXCURSIONS

EL ESCORIAL

The first impression of the Real Monasterio de San Lorenzo de El Escorial is always its vast size. Some 50km (31 miles) northwest of Madrid, this combination of monastery, palace and royal mausoleum was built to celebrate victory against the French in the battle of St Quentin in 1557. Six years later, Felipe II set out to flaunt Spain's roles as rulers of the world and as the bulwark of Roman Catholicism against the forces of the Reformation. It took 21 years to complete and has 1,200 doors, 2,600 windows and some 24km (15 miles) of corridors. The result must have impressed both the king's subjects and his European rivals.

The interior, including the royal apartments, is surprisingly austere, reflecting Felipe II's taste. Highlights include the Nuevos Museos (New Museum of Art), with major works by Titian, Tintoretto, Veronese, Rubens and van Dyck. Among several fine paintings by El Greco are *The Martyrdom of St Maurice* (one of his finest, though Felipe II did not like it) and *The Dream of Felipe II*, portraying the ascetic king at prayer in paradise. The heart of El Escorial is the vast basilica, which is reminiscent of St Peter's in Rome, while the library (one of Felipe II's pet projects) holds an important collection of 15th- and 16th-century books. With its lavish baroque decoration, the pantheon is the burial place of the Spanish royal family. Carlos I was the first to be buried there. Expect crowds on weekends.

EXCURSIONS

Marked by a 150m-high (490ft) cross, the **Valle de los Caídos** (Valley of the Fallen), 9km (5.5 miles) north, is a monument to General Franco and the Falangists (the Spanish Fascists).

El Escorial
☎ 91 890 59 02 and 91 890 59 03   Tue–Sun 10–6 (summer); 10–5 (winter)
Moderate; free Wed for EU citizens   Multilingual audioguides available
Calle Grimaldi 2 ☎ 91 890 53 13

Valle de los Caídos
☎ 91 890 56 11   Tue–Fri 10–6, Sat, Sun 10–7 (summer); 10–5 (winter)
Inexpensive; free Wed for EU citizens   664

EXCURSIONS

MANZANARES EL REAL

In summer, *madrileños* head for the cooler heights of the Sierra de Guadarrama and the town of Manzanares El Real, 47km (29 miles) north of the capital. Legend has it that Felipe II considered establishing El Escorial (➤ 164–165) here. Certainly the 15th-century castle, with its backdrop of the Sierra de Pedriza, is dramatic. Built for the dukes of Infantado, the fortress retains Moorish features such as honeycomb cornices. Explore the quiet gardens bordering the banks of the Rio Manzanares, then head for

EXCURSIONS

the open spaces of **La Pedriza Regional Park,** highly prized for its invigorating mountain air, nature trails, panoramic views, wildlife (Griffin vultures) and the oddly shaped granite boulders littering the hillsides.
www.manzanareselreal.org
🛈 Parque Herrén de la Boni ☎ 639 17 96 02

La Pedriza Regional Park
☎ 91 853 99 78 (La Pedriza info) 🎫 Free
🍴 Café and picnic spots ❓ On weekends and holidays the number of cars allowed into La Pedriza car park is restricted

EL PARDO
Like the Valle de los Caídos (➤ 165), El Pardo has uncomfortable associations with the recent past, as the Palacio del Pardo was Franco's main residence for some 35 years. However, before that, the village was a royal favourite for centuries. Felipe II and Carlos III came to hunt, and added to the comforts of the elegant 16th-century palace, which is now used to entertain foreign heads of state. (The present royal family lives just 5km/3 miles away at the Zarzuela Palace).

Although part of the palace is open, the public rarely comes in numbers. However, the 200 Flemish and Spanish tapestries, as well as paintings by Spanish masters, are of interest.
✉ Carretera El Cristo ☎ 91 376 15 00 🕘 Mon–Sat 10:30–5:45, Sun, public hols 9:30–1:30 (summer); 10:30–5, Sun, public hols 9:55–1:40 (winter)
💷 Inexpensive; free Wed for EU citizens ❓ Guided tours in English

EXCURSIONS

a drive around the Guadarrama Mountains

Lovely in spring and autumn, this scenic drive north through the green Guadarrama Mountains is also a cool escape from Madrid in the height of summer.

Leave Madrid on the A-6; turn onto the M-608 at Collado Villalba. Continue to Manzanares el Real.

The 15th-century castle at Manzanares el Real (➤ 166–167) stands proudly, its battlements, watchtowers and fortifications looking as if they have sprouted from the rock.

Continue on the M-608, turn left on the M-611 for Miraflores de la Sierra.

The road climbs through ranches where massive fighting bulls are bred for the corrida (fight). The quiet is broken only by birdsong. In spring and early summer there are wild flowers. On the side of a steep hill, Miraflores is a perfect stop for lunch, with fine views.

Continue on the M-611.

At the pass of Puerto de la Morchera (1,786m/5,860ft), enjoy even more spectacular views across to snowy peaks – even in June. In summer, you pass bushes of wild roses; in autumn, the oaks turn golden brown. The narrow road twists and turns past *refugios*, stone huts for walkers. Just outside Rascafría is a 14th-century monastery; part of it is now a hotel.

EXCURSIONS

At the village of Rascafría, turn right on to the M-604 and continue to Lozoya.

The small village of Lozoya is another good place to stop and stretch your legs before having lunch or a snack.

Follow signs for the A-1 (the E-05), the motorway south to Madrid.

Distance 175km (108 miles)
Time 4 hours, mountain roads
Start/end Madrid
Lunch Hotel Santa María de El Paular (€€) ✉ N-604, Rascafría
☎ 91 869 10 11

EXCURSIONS

SEGOVIA

The old city of Segovia is surprisingly intact and unspoiled by 20th-century buildings. Standing between the Río Eresma and the Arroyo Clamores, with the Sierra de Guadarrama as a backdrop, the city's strategic importance explains its long history.

Segovia is best known for its Roman aqueduct. You can't miss the two tiers of 163 arches built of precisely cut granite, without mortar. Standing 29m (95ft) above the ground at its highest point, it stretches for 813m (2,667ft); the water that once flowed along the channel started its journey some 15km (9 miles) away. This is an awesome piece of civil engineering; by comparison, the brick-and-mortar city wall looks positively messy.

EXCURSIONS

Pick up a map at the tourist information office on Plaza del Azoguejo and head off to explore the old streets. Follow Calle de Cervantes, where the façade of the Casa de los Picos looks like a studded shield. This delightful street of half-timbered houses with wrought-iron balconies changes name as it winds its way uphill; perhaps that is why locals just call it the Calle Real. At the top are the Plaza Mayor and the 16th-century cathedral. Further along the Calle Real is **El Alcázar.** Looking like Sleeping Beauty's castle, complete with turrets and towers, it stands on top of sheer

cliffs, with commanding views across the plain below. Late on Friday and Saturday nights, the city's ancient monuments are illuminated. No visit is complete without sampling the slow-cooked lamb or *cochinillo* (suckling pig), so tender that only a fork is needed.

www.segoviaturismo.com

🛈 40-min tour on tourist trolley. Mon–Thu, Sun runs on the hour 11–1, 4–6, Fri, Sat 11–1, 4–11 ☎ 925 14 22 74

🛈 Plaza del Azoguejo ☎ 921 46 67 20

🕐 10–8. Also Plaza Mayor 10 ☎ 921 46 03 34

🕐 Daily 9–2, 5–8 🛈 Free guided tours of Segovia start here, Jul–Sep 10, 11, 12 (inner city), 4.30 (outer city)

El Alcázar

✉ Plaza de la Reina Victoria Eugenia ☎ 921 46 07 59; www.alcazardesegovia.com 🕐 10–7 (summer); 10–6 (winter) 💰 Inexpensive

EXCURSIONS

a drive to Segovia and the mountains

This route heads northwest past El Escorial and Segovia, before heading for La Granja and a spectacular mountain pass.

Leave Madrid on the A-6; take the exit for El Escorial. This road becomes the M-505.

The massive palace of El Escorial (➤ 164–165) dominates the old town, with its attractive squares and narrow streets.

EXCURSIONS

From El Escorial, route M-600 to Guadarrama passes the entrance to the Valle de los Caídos (▶ 165) and heads into the tunnel beneath the Puerto de Guadarrama, 1,611m (5,285ft) above sea level. Take the N-603 for Segovia.

Don't be put off by the modern outskirts of Segovia; the old heart of the city has an undeniable charm (▶ 170–171) and is an excellent place to stop for lunch.

From Segovia, the CL-601, signposted Madrid and La Granja, leads up into the hills.

The main attraction in La Granja de San Ildefonso is Felipe V's romantic 18th-century palace, a mini-Versailles. Nearby is the Riofrío Palace, built by Felipe's widow, and the **Real Fábrica de Cristales.** In the 18th century, this factory made spectacular chandeliers and mirrors for royal palaces. Today, the craft has been revived in the factory, school and museum.

From La Granja, the CL-601 climbs through peaceful woods, past signs proclaiming ever-increasing altitudes. Admire the view at Puerto de la Navacerrada, a ski resort right at the tree line (1,880m/6,168ft). Return to Madrid via the M-601, through Navacerrada, and the N-6.

Distance 200km (124 miles)
Time 9 hours with stops, 5 hours without stops
Start/end point Madrid
Lunch Casa Duque (€–€€) ✉ Calle de Cervantes 12, Segovia
☎ 921 46 24 87
Real Fábrica de Cristales
✉ Paseo del Pocillo 1, La Granha de San Ildefonso, Segovia ☎ 921 010 700 🕐 Tue–Fri, Sun, public hols 10–2:45, Sat 11–2, 4–5:45; 15 Jun–15 Sep Sun 10–2, 4–5:45 💰 Inexpensive; free under 12

EXCURSIONS

TOLEDO

Don't miss Toledo. Few cities have such a rich tapestry of art, religion and history. Ironically, a 16th-century painter from Crete is most closely associated with this city, set high on a bluff above the Río Tajo (River Tagus). El Greco (The Greek) painted his greatest works here, including a menacing landscape of the city dominated by its cathedral and fortress. Both still punctuate the skyline of this medieval city, with its steep streets and twisting alleyways.

Toledo is often called the 'city of the three cultures', reflecting the harmony and prosperity enjoyed by Christians, Jews and Muslims during the Middle Ages. The Islamic heritage is recalled in the Moorish architecture, with characteristic keyhole arches and forbidding doors hiding beautiful courtyards. In the Judería (the Jewish quarter), two of the original ten synagogues survive. These were renovated in 1992, along with many houses, five centuries after the expulsion of all Jews from Spain. The cathedral, started in 1226, is one of Spain's largest and after the royal court moved to Madrid in 1560, Toledo remained the country's religious capital.

EXCURSIONS

A mini-lesson in Spanish history, with Roman, Visigoth and Moorish connections, this ancient stronghold became the capital of Castile in 1085. It thrived as a centre of learning, commerce and religious tolerance. Toledo swords and armour were famous throughout Europe. Although there are more than enough museums and churches to admire, the best way to appreciate Toledo is to be there at night after the tourists have left.

❓ 50-min tour through old town on Zocotren tourist trolley; www.zocotren.com. Starts Plaza de Zocodover 🕐 From 11am; also at night, weekends. Leaves on the half-hour (summer); on the hour (winter)

ℹ️ Puerta de Bisagra s/n ☎ 925 22 08 43; www.guiatoledo.com 🕐 Mon–Fri 9–6, Sat 9–7, Sun, public hols 9–3

EXCURSIONS

a walk around Toledo

This atmospheric walk takes in all the important sights. Toledo has steep hills and cobblestone streets, so wear comfortable shoes.

Start at the Plaza de Zocodover.

Through the large Moorish archway under the clock steps lead to the **Museo de Santa Cruz**, a fine museum known for its El Greco paintings. Up the hill on Cuesta Carlos V is the Alcázar fortress.

From the plaza, follow Calle de Comercio. Turn left to the front of the Cathedral.

This enormous Gothic structure is a treasure chest of religious art. The sacristy is hung with works by El Greco, van Dyck and Goya.

Cross the square and follow the alley to the right of the town hall; it narrows into a passageway and you step through a doorway into a tiny square. Turn right onto Calle de El Salvador. Go uphill to Calle de Santo Tomé. Turn left on San Juan de Dios for the Iglesia de Santo Tomé.

Underneath its Moorish tower, the 14th-century **church** houses El Greco's huge painting, *The Burial of the Count of Orgaz*. Across the square, the **Casa-Museo de El Greco** is dedicated to the famous painter.

EXCURSIONS

From here, Calle de San Juan de Dios leads into the Jewish quarter. Continue to the Sinagoga del Tránsito.

With Moorish and Gothic details, this 14th-century synagogue reflects the three cultures of Toledo; the Sephardic Museum explains the traditions of Spanish Jews.

From here, return to the Plaza de Zocodover or wander through more ancient alleyways.

Distance 1km (0.5 miles), hilly
Time 1 hour without stops, 5 hours with stops
Start Plaza de Zocodover
End Sinagoga del Tránsito
Lunch Casa Aurelio (€–€€)
✉ Sinagoga 6 ☎ 925 22 20 97

Museo de Santa Cruz
✉ Calle de Cervantes 3 ☎ 925 22 14 02 ◷ 10–6:30, Sun 10–2
✋ Free

Casa-Museo de El Greco
✉ Calle de Samuel Levi 3 ☎ 925 22 40 46 ◷ Tue–Sat 10–2, 4–6, Sun 10–2 ✋ Inexpensive

EXCURSIONS

HOTELS

Spain has long been famous for its *paradores*, a government-run chain of hotels. These are often converted castles, palaces and monasteries in attractive locations with reasonably priced rooms. The properties have successfully retained the historical character of the building are usually beautifully furnished with antiques and are oases of calm. They also make a point of serving original dishes in their restaurants. Central reservations ☎ 91 516 66 66; www.parador.es.

ALCALA DE HENARES
Hospederîa La Tercia (€€)
Small but charming hotel (10 rooms) situated in a 17th-century building near the university. Comfortable, well equipped rooms, restaurant and terrace.
✉ Calle La Tercia 8 ☎ 91 879 68 00; www.latercia.com

CHINCHÓN
Parador Nacional de Turismo (€€–€€€)
Get away from it all in this converted 15th-century convent. Wander in the gardens, with their pear trees and jasmine, or swim the pool. Elegant restaurant (➤ 180).
✉ Calle de los Huertos 1 ☎ 91 894 08 36; www.parador.es

EL ESCORIAL
Hotel Victoria Palace (€€–€€€)
A grand 4-star hotel with 87 rooms, just 200m (220yds) from the famous monastery-palace. Some rooms have balconies. Swimming pool, restaurants.
✉ Calle de Juan de Toledo 4 ☎ 91 896 98 90; www.hotelvictoriapalace.com

Parilla del Príncipe (€)
A restaurant with rooms (➤ 180) in an 18th-century palace. The 23 bedrooms are simple but comfortable.
✉ Calle de Floridablanca 6 ☎ 91 890 16 11; www.parrillaprincipe.com

EXCURSIONS

SEGOVIA

Ayala Berganza (€€)
A 15th-century palace converted into a stylish, modern 4-star hotel. The look is minimalist, with the ancient walls and arches adding character. Luxurious bedrooms, each decorated in its own style; private parking.

✉ Calle de Carretas 5 ☎ 92 146 04 48; www.partner-hotels.com

Hotel Infanta Isabel (€)
Converted into a hotel in 1992, this lovely old 19th-century building has a wonderful position overlooking the Plaza Mayor. Ask for a room with a balcony so that you can admire the cathedral. The rooms are individually decorated. Good breakfast. An ideal base for discovering Segovia.

✉ Plaza Mayor 12 ☎ 92 146 13 00; www.hotelinfantaisabel.com

Parador de Segovia (€€–€€€)
A 113-room hotel surrounded by trees and lawns, only 3km (2 miles) from Segovia's famous aqueduct. Restaurant, gym, sauna and two swimming pools.

✉ Carretera de Valladolid ☎ 92 144 37 37; www.parador.es

TOLEDO

Hostal del Cardenal (€–€€)
What was once the home of the powerful archbishops of Toledo is now a 27-room hotel. Eighteenth-century touches, such as glazed tiles, remain, as does the lovely garden, interspersed with ponds and ancient walls covered with cascading vines. The restaurant is highly rated.

✉ Paseo de Recaredo 24 ☎ 92 522 49 00; www.hotelcardenal.com

Parador del Conde de Orgaz (€€–€€€)
The best feature of this modern hillside hotel is its sunset views of the city across the river. The restaurant serves local specialities. Renovations are due to finish in 2008.

✉ Paseo de los Cigarrales ☎ 92 522 18 50; www.parador.es

EXCURSIONS

RESTAURANTS

ALCALÁ DE LA HENARES
Hostería del Estudiante (€€)
One of the 15th-century student colleges has been restored and is now a restaurant serving Castilian dishes.
✉ Calle de los Colegios 3 ☎ 91 888 03 30 ⏲ Lunch, dinner. Closed Aug

ARANJUEZ
Casa José (€)
There's nowhere better to eat asparagus and strawberries where they are grown than this high-class restaurant, regarded as the best in town.
✉ Calle de los Abastos 32 ☎ 91 891 14 88 ⏲ Lunch, dinner. Closed Sun dinner, Mon, Aug

CHINCHÓN
Parador Nacional de Turismo (€–€€)
Just off the Plaza Mayor, this converted former convent and cloisters is a delightful oasis of calm and elegance. Fine restaurant, local dishes.
✉ Calle de los Huertos 1 ☎ 91 894 08 36 ⏲ Lunch, dinner

EL ESCORIAL
Parrilla del Príncipe (€–€€)
A restaurant set in an 18th-century palace. Fish dishes make a welcome change from the typical mountain fare of so many restaurants.
✉ Calle de Floridablanca 6 ☎ 91 890 15 48 ⏲ Lunch, dinner

Charoles (€€€)
Classy restaurant famed for its traditional cooking, including the nourishing, slow-cooked stew *cocido madrileño*, recommended by the Spanish gastronomy association (Mon–Fri only). Extensive wine list.
✉ Calle Floridablanca 24 ☎ 91 890 59 75 ⏲ Lunch, dinner.

EXCURSIONS

LA GRANJA DE SAN ILDEFONSO
Restaurante Zaca (€)
Eating here is like eating in a Spanish home, with hearty dishes such as ox tongue and stews. Family-run for 60 years. Worth making a reservation.

✉ Calle de los Embajadores 6 ☎ 92 147 00 87 🕐 Lunch only. Closed last week Jun, 1 week mid-Oct

EL PARDO
La Marquesita (€€)
Game and roast meats are the specialities of this old restaurant near the El Pardo Palace, which was once a hunting lodge. Excellent desserts.

✉ Avenida de la Guardia 29 ☎ 91 376 03 77 🕐 Lunch, dinner

SEGOVIA
La Floresta (€€–€€€)
Eat roast suckling pig in one of the small dining rooms or in the courtyard among a fountain and flowers.

✉ Calle de San Agustín 27 ☎ 921 46 33 14 🕐 Lunch, dinner. Closed Mon dinner

TOLEDO
La Abadía (€–€€)
Next to the Iglesia de San Nicolás, this informal restaurant is in the brick cellar of a 16th-century mansion. Above-average cooking, and unusual *tapas*.

✉ Plaza San Nicolás 3 ☎ 92 525 11 40 🕐 Lunch, dinner

El Casón de los López de Toledo (€€–€€€)
Lamb with figs is among the enterprising dishes served in this former private home, considered one of the most beautiful buildings in Toldeo. Courtyard with plants downstairs; elegant dining-room upstairs.

✉ Calle de la Sillería 3 ☎ 90 219 83 44 🕐 Lunch, dinner. Closed Sun dinner

Index

Abono Paseo del Arte ticket 16
accommodation 103–104, 126–127, 149–150, 178–179
advance passenger information (API) 23
airport and air services 26, 27
Alcalá de Henares 11, 74, 88, 121, 158–159
El Alcázar, Segovia 171
Anís de Chinchón 162
antiques, books and music 108, 151
aqueduct, Segovia 170
Aquasur 70
Aquópolis San Fernando de Henares 70
Aquópolis Villa Nueva de la Cañada 70
Aranjuez 11, 71, 160–161, 163
art galleries 16, 62
arts, crafts, gifts and design 108–109, 128, 151–152
Atletico Madrid 19, 72
Atocha Railway Station 122

banks 32
Barbara of Braganza 135
bars, clubs and live music 64–65, 110–112, 154–155
Basilica de San Francisco el Grande 82–83
Basilica de San Miguel 83, 98
basketball 72
Bernabéu Stadium 19, 60, 66, 121, 134
Bolsa 123
Botín 84–85
breakdowns 29
bullfighting 146–147
Burial of the Sardine ceremony 24, 95
buses 26, 28

cable-car 60
cafés and bars 64–65
Calle de Alcalá 74–75, 88, 123
Calle de los Cuchilleros 98
Calle de Serrano 130
Campo del Moro 60, 76
Capilla del Obispo 89
Capilla de San Isidro 89
car rental 29
Carlos III 100, 121
Casa de América 131, 155
Casa de Campo 73, 76–77

Casa de Cisneros 86
Casa de Correos 100–101
Casa del Labrador, Aranjuez 160, 161
Casa-Museo de El Greco, Toledo 176, 177
Casa Museo de Lope de Vega 85
Casa Natal de Cervantes, Alcalá de Henares 159
Casa de la Panadería 54
Casa de los Picos, Segovia 171
Casa y Torre de Lujanes 86
Casa de Vacas 53
Casa de la Villa 86, 98
Casón del Buen Retiro 44, 115
Catedral de la Almudena 87
Centro Amor de Dios 91
Centro Cultural Conde Duque 131, 155
Centro Cultural de la Villa de Madrid 145, 155
ceramics 66
Cervantes 90, 142, 159
Chicote, Perico 138
children's attractions 70–71
Chillida, Eduardo 138, 148
Chinchón 162–163
Chueca 129
Churriguera, José 89
Círculo de las Bellas Artes 74
climate and seasons 11, 22
Colegiata de San Isidro 87
Colegio Mayor de San Ildefonso, Alcalá de Henares 159
Colón, Cristóbal (Christopher Columbus) 145
concessions 29
consulates 31
Convento de las Carboneras 88, 98
crime 32
cultural centres 131, 145, 155

De Vega, Lope 85
Descalzas Reales (Barfeoot Royal Sister) 37
Discovery Gardens 145
drink driving 29
drinking water 32
drives
Guadarrama Mountains 168–169

Segovia and the Mountains 172–173
south of Madrid 162–163
driving 22, 26, 29
drugs and medicines 31

eating out 18, 58–59, 64–65, 68–69, 104–107, 127, 150, 180–181
Eastern Madrid 113–128
economy 11
Edificio del Banco Central 143
Edificio España 142
Edificio la Estrella 143
Edificio Metrópolis 143
Edificio Villanueva 44
electricity 32
embassies 31
emergency telephone numbers 31
entertainment 110–112, 154–155
El Entierro de la Sardina 24, 95
Ermita de San Antonio de la Florida 24, 77, 132, 148
El Escorial 164–165, 166, 172
Estadio Santiago Bernabéu 19, 60, 66, 121, 134
excursions 156–181
Alcalá de Henares 158–159
Aranjuez 160–161
El Escorial 164–165, 166, 172
Manzanares el Real 166–167
El Pardo 167
Segovia 170–171
Toledo 174–175, 176–177

fans 66
fares 29
Faro de Madrid 60–61
fashion 128, 152–153
Faunia 70
festivals and events 24–25
flamenco 111
food and drink 12–15, 18, 110, 153
see also eating out
football 19, 72, 134
Franco, General 165, 167
fuel 29
Fundación La Caixa 62
Fundación Carlos de Amberes 62
Fundación Juan March 62

182

Fundación Mapfre Vida 62
Fundación Telefónica 62

Galdiano, José Lázaro 40–41
Galerías Piquer 102
galleries 62
geography 10
golf 72
Goya 40, 44, 83, 84, 94, 95, 124, 132, 176
Gran Café Gijón 59, 121
Gran Via 74, 142–143
La Granja de San Ildefonso 172, 173
El Greco 40, 75, 137, 164, 174, 176
Guadarrama Mountains 168–169, 173
Guernica (Picasso) 42, 43

health 23, 31
Hemingway, Ernest 85
Hotel Ritz 59, 77, 122
House of Cows 53

ice-skating 72–73
Iglesia de las Calatravas 75, 88–89
Iglesia de las Salesas 134
Iglesia de San Andrés Apóstol 89, 98
Iglesia de Santa Bárbara 134–135
Iglesia de San José 74
Iglesia de San Pedro el Viejo 98
Iglesia de Santo Tomé, Toledo 176
Iglesia y Convento de las Trinitarias 90
insurance 22, 23

Jardines de Descubrimiento 145
Jardines de Sabatini 77
Jardines de las Vístillas 60
Judería, Toldeo 174

Kilometre 0 100

language 33
leather goods 66, 153–154
leisure facilities 11
Linnaeus 125
Lozoya 169

Madrid Stock Exchange 123
Manzanares el Real 166–167, 168
markets 66, 90–91, 102
medical treatment 23
Mercado Antón Martín 90–91
Mercado de San Miguel 90
Metro 28
Miraflores de la Sierra 168
Monasterio de las Descalzas Reales 36–37
Monasterio de la Encarnación 92
money 30
Morata de Tajuña 162
Monumento al Descubrimiento de América 145
Museo de América 38–39
Museo Arqueológico Nacional 136–137
Museo Cerralbo 137
Museo Chicote 138
Museo de Escultura al Aire Libre 138–139
Museo Lázaro Galdiano 40–41
Museo Nacional de Antropología 115
Museo Nacional de Artes Decorativas 116
Museo Nacional Centro de Arte Reina Sofía 42–43, 60, 121, 122
Museo Naval 117, 123
Museo Picasso – Colección Arias 62
Museo del Prado 44–45, 120, 122
Museo de la Real Academia de Bellas Artes de San Fernando 75, 94–95
Museo Romántico 140–141
Museo de Santa Cruz, Toledo 176, 177
Museo Sorolla 46–47
Museo Taurino 146, 147
Museo Thyssen-Bornemisza 48–49, 60, 121, 122
Museo del Traje 141
Museum of Costume 141
museum opening hours 32

National Archaeological Museum 136–137
national holidays 24
New Museum of Art 164

Northern Madrid 129–155
Nuevos Museos 164

Old Madrid 81–112
opening hours 32

Palacio de Comunicaciones 118–119, 123
Palacio de las Cortes 97
Palacio de Cristal 53, 62
Palacio de Linares 131
Palacio del Pardo 167
Palacio de la Prensa 142
Palacio Real, Aranjuez 160, 161
Palacio Real, Madrid 19, 50–51
Palacio de Velázquez 53
Palacio de Villahermosa 48
paradores 140, 178
El Pardo 167
Parque de Atracciones 71
Parque Florida 40
Parque de la Montaña 77
Parque del Oeste 77
Parque del Retiro 52–53, 76, 101
Paseo de la Castellana, 120, 121
Paseo del Estanque 52
Paseo del Pintor Rosales 77
Paseo del Prado 120, 122–123
Paseo de Recoletos 25, 120, 121
paseos 10, 113, 120–121, 122–123
passports and visas 22
La Pedriza Regional Park 167
personal safety 32
pharmacies 31, 32
Plaza de Cascorro 102
Plaza de la Cibeles 120, 123, 145
Plaza de Colón 145
Plaza de Independencia 121
Plaza Mayor 54–55, 98, 99
Plaza de la Paja 98
Plaza de Toros de Las Ventas 146–147
Plaza de Vázquez de Mella 77
Plaza de la Villa 86
police 31, 32
population 11
La Posada de la Villa 98
postal services 31
Prado *see* Museo del Prado

public transport 27–28
Puerta de Alcalá 101, 121, 123, 145
Puerta del Sol 25, 75, 100–101, 145
Puerta de Toledo 101
Puerto de Guadarrama 173
Puerto de la Morchera 168
Puerto de la Navacerrada 173

Rascafría 168–169
El Rastro (Rastro flea market) 32, 66, 102
Real Armería 51
Real Fábrica de Cristales 173
Real Fábrica de Tapices 124–125
Real Farmacia 51
Real Jardín Botánico 77, 121, 122, 125
Real Madrid 60, 121, 134
Real Monasterio de San Lorenzo de El Escorial (El Escorial) 164–164
Retiro Park 52–53
Riofrío Palace 173
Ritz see Hotel Ritz
Roman aqueduct 51
La Rosaleda 53, 77
Royal Academy 94–95
Royal Armoury 51
Royal Pharmacy 51

Safari de Madrid 71
Sala de Exposiciones del Alcalá 62
Sala de Exposiciones – Canal de Isabel II 62

Sala de Exposiciones del Círculo de Bellas Artes 62
Salamanca 129, 130
San Ginés 75
San Isidro 24, 54, 89, 98
seat belts 29
Segovia 170–171, 172, 173
senior citizens 29
Sephardic Museum, Toledo 177
shopping 16, 18, 32, 66, 102, 108–110, 128, 151–154
Sierra de Pedriza 166
Sierra de Guadarrama 11, 166, 168–169, 170
Sinagoga del Tránsito, Toledo 177
La Sirena Varada 138
skiing 73
soccer 19, 72, 134
Sorolla, Joaquín 46–47, 95
souvenirs 66
speed limits 29
sport 72–73
Stock Exchange 118, 123
Strawberry Train 71, 160
students and young travellers 29
sun advice 31
Sunday morning activities 16
swimming pools 60, 73

tapas 13–14, 68–69
tapestry factory 124–125
taxis 28
Teatro Monumental 112
Teatro Real 60, 75, 112
Teatro de la Zarzuela 112
Teleférico 60, 76, 77, 148
Telefónica 142, 148

telephones 31
Templete de la Musica 52
terrazas 9, 18, 121
theatre, cinema, music and dance 112, 155
time differences 23
tipping 30
Toledo 163, 174–175, 176–177
Torre de Madrid 142
tourist offices 23, 30
traffic offences 29
trains 26, 27
Tren de la Fresa 71, 160
TroCortesiano Codex 38
Tudela Codex 39

Universidad Complutense 158

Valle de los Caidos (Valley of the Fallen) 165, 167, 173
Vega, Lope de 85, 90
Vicente Calderón stadium 19
views of Madrid 60–61
Villaconejos 163

walks
  Calle de Alcalá 74–75
  Gran Vía 142–143
  Medieval Madrid 98–99
  Paseo del Prado 122–123
  Toledo 176–177
Warnerbros Park 71
waterparks 70
websites 23
wine 15

Xanadu 73

Zarzuela Palace 50, 167

Street Index

Abada, Calle **17H**
Abtao, Calle de **24M**
Academia, Calle de la **20K**
Acuerdo, Calle del **6E**
Aduana, Calle de la **17J**
Aguas, Calle las **15L**
Aguila, Calle del **15L**
Agustin de Betancourt, Calle **9A**
Alameda, Calle de la **19K**
Alberto Aguilera, Calle **5D**
Alcalá, Calle de **22H**
Alcalde, Calle del **24J**
Alfonso XII, Calle de **21K**
Almadén, Calle **19L**
Almagro, Calle de **10D**
Almirante, Calle del **20H**
Alonso Cano, Calle de **8A**
Alonso Martínez, Plaza **9E**
Amado Nervo, Calle **24L**
Amaniél, Calle de **6F**
Amparo, Calle del **18M**
Andrés Mellado, Calle de **5C**
Andrés Torrejon, Calle **22L**
Angel, Calle de **15L**
Angel, Plaza de **15L**
Angel Caído, Glorieta del **22L**
Angel Caído, Puerta del **21L**
Angel Ganivet, Calle **24L**
Aniceto, Calle de **2F**
Aniceto Marinas, Calle de **1E**
Antonio Acuña, Calle **23H**
Antonio Bienvenida, Calle **24L**
Antonio Grillo, Calle **16G**
Antonio Maura, Calle de **20J**
Antonio Pérez, Calle **12A**
Antón Martín, Plaza de **18K**
Arapiles, Calle de **6D**
Arco de la Victoria, Avenida **2B**
Arenal, Calle de **17J**
Argensola, Calle de **9F**

Argentina, Paseo de la **21J**
Argenzuela, Calle la **16M**
Argumosa, Calle de **19M**
Armería, Plaza de la **15J**
Arquitecto López Otero, Calle **1A**
Arrieta, Calle de **16J**
Atocha, Calle de **18K**
Atocha, Ronda de **19M**
Augusto Figueroa, Calle de **18H**
Avemaría, Calle del **18L**
Ayala, Calle de **11E**
Azorin, Glorieta **13K**
Bailén, Calle de **15K**
Bárbara de Braganza, Calle **20G**
Barco, Calle del **18G**
Barquillo, Calle del **19G**
Beatriz Galindo, Calle **15K**
Belén, Calle de **9F**
Beneficencia, Calle **8E**
Benito Gutiérrez, Calle de **3D**
Bilbao, Glorieta **7E**
Blasco de Garay, Calle **5D**
Boccherini, Glorieta **14K**
Boix y Morer, Calle **6B**
Bolivia, Paseo **22H**
Bolsa, Calle de **17K**
Bravo Murillo, Calle de **7C**
Bretón de los Herreros, Calle **9B**
Buen Suceso, Calle de **4E**
Cabeza, Calle de la **18K**
Cadarso, Calle **15H**
Calatrava, Calle de **15L**
Callao, Plaza de **17H**
Calvario, Calle de **17L**
Camoens Alcántara, Paseo de **2D**
Campoamor, Calle **9E**
Canovas del Castillo, Plaza **19J**
Caracas, Calle de **9D**
Cardenal Cisneros, Calle **7D**

Cardenal Cisneros, Plaza de **2B**
Carlos Arniches, Calle **16M**
Carmen, Plaza de **17H**
Carranza, Calle **7E**
Carretas, Calle de **17J**
Casino, Calle del **17M**
Castellana, Paseo de la **10D**
Castelló, Calle de **12D**
Castillion de la Plana, Calle **11B**
Cava Baja, Calle de la **16K**
Cavanilles, Calle de **24M**
Cea Bermúdez, Calle de **5B**
Cebada, Plaza de la **16L**
Cerrada, Puerta **16K**
Cervantes, Calle de **19K**
Chopera, Paseo de la **21L**
Churruca, Calle de **8E**
Cibeles, Plaza de **20H**
Ciudad de Barcelona, Avenida de la **21M**
Ciudad de Plasencia, Paseo **14K**
Claudio Coello, Calle de **11E**
Claudio Moyano, Calle **20L**
Colombia, Paseo de **22H**
Colón, Plaza de **10F**
Comandante Fortea, Calle del **1F**
Complutense, Avenida **2A**
Concepción Jeronima, Calle **17K**
Conde Aranda, Calle del **21H**
Conde de Cartagena, Calle **24L**
Conde Duque, Calle de **6E**
Corrala, Plaza la **17L**
Corredera Baja de San Pablo, Calle **17H**
Cortes, Plaza de las **19J**
Costa Rica, Plaza **22H**
Covarrubias, Calle de **9E**
Cristino Martos, Plaza **5F**
Cristóbal Bordiú, Calle de **7A**

Cristo Rey, Plaza **4B**
Cruz, Calle de la **18J**
Cruz Verde, Calle **16G**
Cruz Verde, Plaza **15K**
Cuchilleros, Calle **16K**
Daoiz, Calle **7E**
Desengaño, Calle del **17H**
Diego de León, Calle **12C**
Divino Pastor, Calle del **7E**
Doce de Octubre, Calle del **24J**
Doctor Castelo, Calle del **24H**
Doménico Scarlatti, Calle **4A**
Donoso Cortés, Calle de **6C**
Don Pedro, Calle **15K**
Don Ramón de la Cruz, Calle de **12E**
Dr Marañón, Plaza **10B**
Dr Piga, Calle **18L**
Duque de Fernán Núñez, Paseo del **23K**
Duque de Sesto, Calle de **24H**
Echegaray, Calle de **18K**
Eduardo Dato, Paseo de **9D**
Eloy Gonzalo, Calle **8C**
Embajadores, Calle de **17M**
Embajadores, Glorieta de **17M**
Emilio Castelar, Glorieta **10C**
Emperador Carlos V, Plaza del **20L**
Escalinata, Calle de la **16J**
Escosura, Calle **6C**
Espalter, Calle de **20K**
España, Plaza de **15G**
España, Puerta **21J**
Espateros, Calle de **17J**
Espíritu Santo, Calle **7F**
Espoz y Mina, Calle **18J**
Espronceda, Calle de **9B**
Estrella, Calle la **17H**
Evaristo San Miguel, Calle **4E**
Factor, Calle de **15J**
Fé, Calle la **18L**

Feijoo, Calle **7C**
Felipe II, Avenida **24G**
Felipe IV, Calle de **20K**
Fernandez de la Hoz, Calle **9B**
Fernández de los Ríos, Calle de **5C**
Fernando El Católico, Calle **5C**
Fernando El Santo, Calle **10E**
Fernando VI, Calle **9F**
Fernán González, Calle de **24H**
Ferraz, Calle de **3D**
Filipinas, Avenida de **6B**
Florida, Paseo de la **13H**
Fomento, Calle del **16H**
Fortuny, Calle de **10C**
Francisco Morano, Plaza **14M**
Fúcar, Calle de **19K**
Fuencarral, Calle de **7E**
Galicia, Plaza **22H**
Galileo, Calle de **6C**
Garcia Paredes, Calle **9C**
Garcilaso, Calle **8D**
Gaztambide, Calle de **4C**
General Alvarez de Castro, Calle **7C**
General Arrando, Calle del **9D**
General Castaños, Calle **9F**
General Martinez Campos, Paseo **9C**
General Oráa, Calle del **12C**
General Vara de Rey, Plaza **16L**
Génova, Calle de **10E**
Ginés, Plaza **17J**
G Miró, Plaza **15K**
Gobernador, Calle del **19K**
Goya, Calle de **12F**
Gran Capitán, Glorieta **6D**
Gran Via **18H**
Granada, Calle de **23M**
Granada, Puerta **23K**
Granado, Plaza **15K**

Gravina, Calle **19G**
Guatemala, Plaza de **22J**
Gutenberg, Calle de **23M**
Guzmán El Bueno, Calle de **5C**
Guzmán El Bueno, Glorieta **5B**
Hermosilla, Calle de **12E**
Hernani, Puerta **21H**
Hilarión Eslava, Calle de **4C**
Hileras, Calle de **16J**
Honduras, Plaza de **22J**
Hortaleza, Calle de **18G**
Huertas, Calle de las **19K**
Humilladero, Calle del **16L**
Humilladero, Plaza **16K**
Ibiza, Calle de **24J**
Illustración, Calle **14H**
Imperial, Paseo **14K**
Independencia, Plaza de la **21H**
Independencia, Puerta **21H**
Infantas, Calle de las **19H**
Irún, Calle de **14H**
Isaac Peral, Calle **4C**
Jacinto Benavente, Plaza **17K**
Jardines, Calle de **18J**
Jenner, Calle **10D**
Jesús, Plaza **19K**
Jesús del Valle, Calle **7F**
Jesús Montoya, Calle **5A**
Jesús y Maria, Calle **17L**
Joaquin Costa, Calle de **12A**
Joaquin Maria López, Calle de **4B**
Jordán, Calle del **7D**
Jorge Juan, Calle de **22G**
Jorge Manrique, Calle **10A**
José Abascal, Calle **8B**
José Ortega y Gasset, Calle **11D**
Juan Alvarez, Calle **4E**
Juan Bravo, Calle de **12D**
Juan de Herrera, Avenida **1B**
Juan de Mena, Calle **20J**

Juan de Urbieta, Calle **24L**
Juan Duque, Calle de **14K**
Juanelo, Calle de **17L**
Juan Vigón, Calle de **5A**
Juan Zorilla, Plaza **7A**
Julian Gayarre, Calle de **22M**
Julián Romea, Calle **4A**
Julio Rey Pastor, Calle **24L**
Lagasca, Calle de **11E**
Larra, Calle de **8E**
Lavapiés, Calle de **17L**
Lavapiés, Plaza **18L**
Lealtad, Plaza de la **20J**
Leganitos, Calle de **16H**
León, Calle de **18K**
Limón, Calle **6E**
Linneo, Calle de **13K**
Lombia, Calle de **24G**
Lope de Rueda, Calle de **23H**
Lopez de Hoyos, Calle de **11B**
López de Hoyos, Glorieta **12B**
Luchana, Calle de **8D**
Lucio del Valle, Calle **6B**
Luisa Fernanda, Calle **5E**
Luis de Góngora, Calle **19G**
Luna, Calle de la **17H**
Madera, Calle de la **17G**
Madrazo, Calle de los **19J**
Madrid, Puerta de **22H**
Maestro, Glorieta **2D**
Maestro Villa, Plaza **21H**
Magallanes, Calle de **7C**
Magdalena, Calle de **18K**
Maiquez, Calle de **24H**
Maldonado, Calle de **12C**
Manuela Malasaña, Calle **7E**
Manuel Silvela, Calle **8E**
Manzana, Calle **16G**
Manzanares, Avenida del **13L**
Manzanares, Calle de **14K**
María de Molina, Calle **11B**

Mariano de Cavia, Plaza **23M**
Marqués de la Ensenada, Calle de **10F**
Marqués de Monistrol, Paseo del **1F**
Marqués de Pontejós, Calle de **21K**
Marqués de Santa Ana, Calle **7F**
Marqués de Urquijo, Calle **4D**
Marqués Riscal, Calle **10D**
Martín de los Heros, Calle **3D**
Martin Fierro, Avenida **1C**
Mártires de Alcalá, Calle **5E**
Matute, Plaza de **18K**
Mayor, Calle **17J**
Mayor, Plaza **16J**
Mediterráneo, Avenida del **24M**
Mejía Lequerica, Calle **8E**
Méjico, Avenida **21H**
Melancólicos, Paseo de los **14K**
Meléndez Valdés, Calle **5D**
Méndez Alvaro, Calle de **20M**
Mendizábal **4E**
Menéndez y Pelayo, Avenida de **23J**
Menorca, Calle de **24H**
Mesón, Calle del **17L**
Miguel Angel, Calle de **10C**
Miguel Servet, Calle **18M**
Mira el Río Baja, Calle **16M**
Mira el Sol, Calle **17M**
Modesto Lafuente, Calle de **9A**
Moncloa, Plaza de la **4C**
Montalbán, Calle de **20J**
Monte Esquinza, Calle de **10E**
Monteleón, Calle **7D**
Montera, Calle de la **17J**
Moratín, Calle de **19K**
Moreno Nieto, Calle **14K**

Moret, Paseo de **3C**
Moreto, Calle de **20K**
Murcia, Calle de **20M**
Murillo, Plaza de **20K**
Murillo, Puerta **21K**
Narciso Serra, Calle **23M**
Narváez, Calle de **24H**
Nazaret, Avenida de **24L**
Nicaragua, Plaza **21J**
Nicasio Gallego, Calle de **8E**
Núñez de Balboa, Calle **12C**
O'Donnell, Calle de **24H**
Olavide, Plaza de **8D**
Olid, Calle **7D**
Olivar, Calle del **18L**
Olmo, Calle del **18K**
Orellana, Calle de **9F**
Oriente, Plaza de **15J**
Pablo Aranda, Calle **11A**
Pablo Iglesias, Avenida de **7A**
Pacifico, Puerta del **23L**
Padilla, Calle de **12D**
Palafox, Calle de **8D**
Palma, Calle de la **7E**
Paloma, Calle de la **15L**
Paredes **17L**
Pedro de Valdivia, Calle de **11B**
Pelayo, Calle de **9F**
Pez, Calle del **17G**
Piamonte, Calle de **19G**
Pinar, Calle de **11B**
Pintor Rosales, Paseo **3E**
Pintor Sorolla, Glorieta **8C**
Pío Baroja, Calle de **24K**
Plateria Martinez, Plaza **19K**
Poeta Esteban Villegas, Calle **22L**
Pontejos, Plaza **17J**
Ponzano, Calle de **8B**
Pozas, Calle de **6F**
Prado, Calle del **18K**
Prado, Paseo del **20L**
Preciados, Calle de **17J**
Prim, Calle de **20H**
Princesa, Calle de la **5F**

Principe, Calle del **18K**
Puerta de Hierro, Avenida **1A**
Puerta del Sol, Plaza **17J**
Puerta de Toledo, Glorieta **15M**
Quevedo, Glorieta de **7C**
Quintana, Calle de **4E**
Rafael Calvo, Calle de **10C**
Raimundo Lulio, Calle de **8D**
Recoletos, Paseo de **20H**
Redondilla, Calle de **15K**
Reina, Calle de la **18H**
Reina Cristina, Paseo **22M**
República de Cuba, Paseo **22K**
Rey, Paseo del **14H**
Rey, Puente del **13J**
Rey Francisco, Calle del **4E**
Reyes, Calle los **6F**
Reyes Católicos, Avenida de los **4B**
Reyes Magos, Calle de **24L**
Ribera de Curtidores, Calle **16L**
Ribera del Manzanares, Calle **1E**
Río, Calle del **15H**
Ríos Rosas, Calle de **7A**
Rodas, Calle de **17L**
Rodriguez San Pedro, Calle **5D**
Romero Robledo, Calle **3D**
Rubén Darío, Glorieta **10D**
Ruiz, Calle de **7E**
Ruiz Jiménez, Glorieta **7E**
Ruperto Chapi, Paseo de **1D**
Sacramento, Calle de **16K**
Sagasta, Calle de **8E**
Sagunto, Calle **8C**
Salítre, Calle del **18L**
Salón del Estanque, Paseo **21J**
San Andrés, Calle de **7E**
San Andrés, Plaza **16K**
San Bartolomé, Calle **18H**
San Bernardino, Calle **6F**
San Bernardo, Calle de **7D**
San Buenaventura, Calle **15K**
San Dimas, Calle **6E**
Sandoval, Calle de **7D**
San Francisco de Sales, Paseo **4B**
San Francisco, Gran via de **15L**
San Francisco, Plaza **15L**
San Isidro Labrador, Calle **15L**
San Jerónimo, Carrera de **19J**
San Juan de la Cruz, Plaza **9A**
San Lorenzo, Calle **8F**
San Marcos, Calle de **19H**
San Martín, Calle **17H**
San Martin, Plaza **16J**
San Mateo, Calle **8E**
San Miguel, Plaza **16J**
San Nicolás, Calle **15J**
Santa Ana, Calle **16L**
Santa Ana, Plaza de **18K**
Santa Brigida, Calle **8F**
Santa Cruz de Marcenado, Calle **5E**
Santa Engracia, Calle de **9D**
Santa Feliciana, Calle **8D**
Santa Isabel, Calle de **19L**
Santa Maria de la Cabeza, Paseo de **19M**
Santa María, Calle **19K**
Santander, Calle de **6A**
Santiago, Calle **16J**
Santísima Trinidad, Calle **8C**
Santo Domingo, Plaza **16H**
Santovenia, Calle de **1E**
San Vicente, Cuesta de **15H**
San Vicente, Glorieta **13H**
San Vicente Ferrer, Calle **7F**
Sardana, Glorieta **22J**
Sebastian Elcano, Calle **19M**
Segovia, Calle de **14K**
Segovia, Puente de **13K**
Senda del Rey, Calle **1D**
Séneca, Avenida de **1C**
Serrano, Calle de **11D**
Serrano Anguita, Calle de **8E**
Sevilla, Glorieta **22H**
Sombrerete, Calle de **17L**
Tabernillas, Calle **15L**
Tesoro, Calle del **7F**
Tetuán, Calle de **17J**
Tirso de Molina, Plaza **17K**
Toledo, Calle de **16K**
Toledo, Ronda de **17M**
Torija, Calle de **16H**
Torrecilla del Leal, Calle **18L**
Trafalgar, Calle **8D**
Tribulete, Calle de **18L**
Tutor. Calle de **4D**
Uruguay, Paseo **23K**
Valderribas, Calle de **23M**
Valencia, Calle **18M**
Valencia, Ronda de **18M**
Valladolid, Avenida de **1E**
Valle, Avenida del **4A**
Vallehermoso, Calle de **6C**
Valverde, Calle de **18G**
Velázquez, Calle de **12D**
Veneras, Calle de **16H**
Venezuela, Paseo de **22J**
Ventura Rodríguez, Calle **4F**
Vergara, Calle de **16J**
Villa, Plaza de **16K**
Villanueva, Calle de **22H**
Virgen del Puerto, Paseo de la **13K**
Viriato, Calle de **9C**
Vitruvio, Calle de **10A**
Vizcaya, Calle de **19M**
Zorilla, Calle de **19J**
Zurbano, Calle de **10B**
Zurbarán, Calle de **10E**
Zurita, Calle de **19L**

Acknowledgements

The Automobile Association wishes to thank the following photographers for their assistance in the preparation of this book.

Abbreviations for the picture credits are as follows – (t) top; (b) bottom; (l) left; (r) right; (c) centre; (AA) AA World Travel Library

4l Plaza de Toros de las Ventas, AA/M Chaplow; **4c** Bus stop, AA/M Chaplow; **4r** Palacio de Cristal, AA/M Chaplow; **5l** Plaza de Isabel II, T Oliver; **5c** Calle de Serrano, AA/R Strange; **5r** Aranjuez Palace Gardens, J Edmanson; **6/7** Plaza de Toros de las Ventas, AA/M Chaplow; **8/9** Corral de la Morrie Flamenco Show, AA/M Jourdan; **10/11t** Plaza Mayor, AA/M Chaplow; **10cr** Matador, AA/M Jourdan; **10bl** Corral de la Morrie Flamenco Show, AA/M Jourdan; **10br** Stained glass, Monasterio el Escoral, AA/M Jourdan; **11cl** Statue of Alfonso XIII in El Retiro Park, AA/M Chaplow; **11bl** Palacio Real, AA/M Chaplow; **12/13t** Ferpal food market, AA/M Jourdan; **12bl** Café, Plaza Mayor, AA/M Chaplow; **12/13bc** Mercado de San Miguel, AA/M Chaplow; **13t** Rice dish, AA/M Jourdan; **13br** Olives, AA/M Chaplow; **14tl** Boquerones en Vinagre, AA/M Chaplow; **14/15b** Café de Oriente, in Plaza de Oriente, AA/M Chaplow; **15tl** Food on sale, Calle de Serrano, AA/M Chaplow; **15tr** Legs of ham, Ferpal, AA/M Jourdan; **16** Museo del Prado, AA/M Jourdan; **17** El Rastro market, AA/M Jourdan; **18t** Plaza Espana, AA/M Jourdan; **19tr** Bernabeu Stadium, AA/M Chaplow; **19cr** Hot chocolate and churros, AA/M Chaplow; **19br** Changing the Guard, Palacio Real, AA/M Jourdan; **20/21** Bus stop, AA/M Chaplow; **25** Corral de la Morrie Flamenco Show, AA/M Jourdan; **27t** Bus stop, AA/M Chaplow; **27b** Estachion de Atocha, AA/M Chaplow; **28** Taxi, AA/M Chaplow; **31** Post box, AA/M Jourdan; **34/35** Palacio de Cristal, AA/M Chaplow; **36/37t** Monasterio de las Descalzas Reales, AA/R Strange; **36/37b** Monasterio de las Descalzas Reales, AA/M Chaplow; **38l** Museo de America, AA/R Strange; **38/39c** Museo de America, AA/R Strange; **41** Museo Lázaro Galdiano, AA/R Strange; **42** Museo Nacional Centro de Arte Reina Sofia, AA/M Jourdan; **43** Museo Nacional Centro de Arte Reina Sofía, AA/M Chaplow; **44** Museo del Prado, AA/M Chaplow; **45c** Museo del Prado, AA/M Jourdan; **45b** Museo del Prado, AA/M Jourdan; **46/47t** Museo Sorolla, AA/R Strange; **46b** Museo Sorolla, AA/R Strange; **48bl** Museo Thyssen-Bornemisza, AA/M Chaplow; **49** Museo Thyssen-Bornemisza, AA/M Chaplow; **50/51b** Palacio Real, AA/M Chaplow; **51tl** Capilla Real, AA/M Jourdan; **52** Parque del Retiro, AA/M Jourdan; **53** Parque del Retiro, AA/M Chaplow; **54** Plaza Mayor, AA/M Chaplow; **55** Statue of Felipe III, Plaza Mayor, AA/M Chaplow; **56-57** Architectural detail, Plaza de Isabel II, T Oliver; **58** El Espejo, AA/M Chaplow; **60-61** Faro de Madrid, AA/R Strange; **62/63** Círculo de Bellas Artes, AA/M Chaplow; **65** Plaza San Andreas, AA/M Chaplow; **67** Fans, AA/M Chaplow; **68** Tapas, AA/M Chaplow; **70/71** Clown, AA/M Chaplow; **73** Skiing, Photodisc; **74** Iglesia de las Calatravas, AA/M Chaplow; **75t** Iglesia de San Ginés, AA/M Chaplow; **75b** Plaza de Isabel II, AA/R Strange; **76** Grounds of Palacio Real, AA/M Jourdan; **78/79** Window display, Calle de Serrano, AA/R Strange; **81** Statue of Carlos III, Puerta del Sol, AA/M Chaplow; **82** San Francisco el Grande, AA/R Strange; **83br** Basilica de San Miguel, AA/M Chaplow; **84/85t** Restaurante Sobrino de Botin, AA/M Chaplow; **84b** Restaurante Sobrino de Botin, AA/M Chaplow; **86/87** Catedral de la Almudena, AA/R Strange; **88/89** Iglesia de las Calatravas, AA/M Chaplow; **90** Fishmonger, AA/M Chaplow; **91t** Butcher, AA/M Chaplow; **91b** Legs of ham, AA/M Jourdan; **92** Monasterio de la Encarnacion, AA/M Chaplow; **93** Monasterio de la Encarnacion, AA/M Chaplow; **94/95t** Museo de la Real Academia de Bellas Artes de San Fernando, AA/J Edmanson; **94b** Museo de la Real Academia de Bellas Artes de San Fernando, AA/J Edmanson; **96** Palacio de las Cortes, AA/M Chaplow; **98** Plaza de la Paja, AA/M Chaplow; **99t** Casa de la Panaderia, Plaza Mayor, AA/M Chaplow; **99b** Plaza Mayor, AA/M Chaplow; **100cl** 'kilometro cero', Origin de las Carreteras Radiales, Puerta del Sol, AA/R Strange; **100/101** Metro, Puerta del Sol, AA/R Strange; **101tr** Statue of a bear and a madroño tree (emblem of Madrid), Puerta del Sol, AA/R Strange; **102** El Rastro Market, AA/M Jourdan; **113** Palm Garden, Estachion de Atocha, AA/M Chaplow; **114/115c** Cason del Buen Retiro, AA/M Chaplow; **116/117** Museo Naval, courtesy of Museo Naval, Madrid; **118/119** Plaza de la Cibeles, AA/M Chaplow; **120/121** Puerta de Alcalá, AA/R Strange; **122c** Atocha Station, AA/R Strange; **122b** Atocha Station, AA/R Strange; **123t** Statue of Neptune, Plaza Canovas del Castillo, AA/R Strange; **124** Real Fábrica de Tapices, AA/M Chaplow; **125t** Real Fábrica de Tapices, AA/M Chaplow; **125b** Real Jardin Botanico, AA/M Jourdan; **129** Plaza de España, AA/M Jourdan; **130** Calle de Serrano, AA/M Chaplow; **131** Palacio de Linares, AA/R Strange; **133** Ermita de San Antonio de la Florida, AA/M Chaplow; **135** Iglesia de las Salesas Reales, AA/R Strange; **136** Museo Arqueológico Nacional, AA/J Edmanson; **138tl** Museo Chicote, AA/M Chaplow; **139** Museo de Escultura al Aire Libre Exhibit, dk/Alamy; **140/141** Salon de Baile, Museo Romántico, AA/M Chaplow; **142** Statue of Don Quixote and Sancho Panza, by Teodoro Ansagasti and Mateo Inurria, AA/R Strange; **143t** Plaza de España, AA/M Jourdan; **143b** Gran Vía, AA/R Strange; **144/145** Cibeles fountain, AA/M Jourdan; **146bl** Matador, AA/M Jourdan; **146/147t** Plaza de Toros de las Ventas, AA/R Strange; **147r** Spectators, Plaza de Toros de Las Ventas, AA/M Jourdan; **148t** Teleférico, AA/M Chaplow; **156/157** The Aranjuez Palace Gardens, AA/J Edmanson; **158/159t** Alcalá de Henares, AA/J Edmanson; **158/159b** Alcalá de Henares, AA/J Edmanson; **159tr** Alcalá de Henares, AA/J Edmanson; **160/161** Aranjuez, AA/J Edmanson; **162** Plaza Mayor, Chinchón, AA/J Edmanson; **163t** Chinchón, AA/J Edmanson; **163c** Toledo, AA/J Edmanson; **164/165** El Escorial, AA/M Chaplow; **166/167** Manzanares El Real, AA/P Enticknap; **168/169** Miraflores de la Sierra, AA/M Chaplow; **170b** Roman aqueduct, Segovia, AA/M Chaplow; **171t** Segovia, AA/M Chaplow; **171b** El Alcázar, AA/P Enticknap; **172b** El Escorial, AA/P Enticknap; **174t** Alcázar, Toledo, AA/M Chaplow; **174/175b** Toledo, AA/M Chaplow; **176cl** Toledo Cathedral, AA/M Chaplow; **176/177c** Plaza de Zocodover, AA/M Chaplow..

Every effort has been made to trace the copyright holders, and we apologise in advance for any unintentional omissions or errors. We would be pleased to apply any corrections in any following edition of this publication.

Sight locator index

This index relates to the maps on the cover. We have given map references to the main sights in the book. Some sights may not be plotted on the maps.

Alcalá de Henares
Aranjuez
Basílica de San Francisco el Grande **15L**
Basílica de San Miguel **16K**
Botín **16K**
Calle de Serrano **11A–21H**
Casa de América **20H**
Casa Museo de Lope de Vega **19K**
Casa de la Villa **16J**
Casón del Buen Retiro **20K**
Catedral de la Almudena **15J**
Centro Cultural Conde Duque **5E**
Colegiata de San Isidro **17K**
Convento de las Carboneras **16J**
Ermita de San Antonio de la Florida **2F**
El Escorial
Estadio Santiago Bernabéu **10A (off map)**
Iglesia de las Calatravas **18J**
Iglesia de San Andrés Apóstol **15K**
Iglesia de Santa Bárbara **19G**

Iglesia y Convento de las Trinitarias **19K**
Manzanares El Real
Mercado Antón Martín **18K**
Monasterio de las Descalzas Reales **17J**
Monasterio de la Encarnación **15H**
Museo de América **3B**
Museo Arqueológico Nacional **20G**
Museo Cerralbo **15G**
Museo Chicote **18H**
Museo de Escultura al Aire Libre **11D**
Museo Lázaro Galdiano **11C**
Museo Nacional de Antropología **21L**
Museo Nacional de Artes Decorativas **20J**
Museo Nacional Centro de Arte Reina Sofía **19L**
Museo Naval **20J**
Museo del Prado **20K**
Museo de la Real Academia de Bellas Artes de San Fernando **18J**

Museo Romántico **8E**
Museo Sorolla **10C**
Museo Thyssen-Bornemisza **19J**
Museo del Traje **1B**
Palacio del Comunicaciones **20J**
Palacio de las Cortes **19J**
Palacio Real **15J**
El Pardo
Parque del Retiro **22K**
The Paseos **10A–20L**
Plaza de la Cibeles **20H**
Plaza de Colón **10F**
Plaza Mayor **16J**
Plaza de Toros de las Ventas **24G (off map)**
Puerta de Alcalá **21H**
Puerta del Sol **17J**
Puerta de Toledo **15M**
El Rastro **16L**
Real Fábrica de Tapices **22M**
Real Jardín Botánico **20L**
Segovia
Teleférico **2E**
Telefónica **18H**
Toledo

Dear Reader

Your comments, opinions and recommendations are very important to us. Please help us to improve our travel guides by taking a few minutes to complete this simple questionnaire.

You do not need a stamp (unless posted outside the UK). If you do not want to cut this page from your guide, then photocopy it or write your answers on a plain sheet of paper.

Send to: **The Editor, AA World Travel Guides, FREEPOST SCE 4598, Basingstoke RG21 4GY.**

Your recommendations...

We always encourage readers' recommendations for restaurants, nightlife or shopping – if your recommendation is used in the next edition of the guide, we will send you a **FREE AA Guide** of your choice from this series. Please state below the establishment name, location and your reasons for recommending it.

_____
_____
_____
_____
_____

Please send me **AA Guide** _____

About this guide...

Which title did you buy?
   AA _____
Where did you buy it? _____
When? m m / y y
Why did you choose this guide? _____
_____
_____
_____

Did this guide meet your expectations?

Exceeded ☐   Met all ☐   Met most ☐   Fell below ☐

Were there any aspects of this guide that you particularly liked? _____
_____
_____

continued on next page...

Is there anything we could have done better? _____
_____
_____
_____

About you...
Name (*Mr/Mrs/Ms*) _____
Address _____
_____
_____ Postcode _____

Daytime tel nos _____
Email _____

Please only give us your mobile phone number or email if you wish to hear from us about other products and services from the AA and partners by text or mms, or email.

Which age group are you in?
Under 25 ☐   25–34 ☐   35–44 ☐   45–54 ☐   55–64 ☐   65+ ☐

How many trips do you make a year?
Less than one ☐   One ☐   Two ☐   Three or more ☐

Are you an AA member? Yes ☐   No ☐

About your trip...
When did you book? m m / y y   When did you travel? m m / y y

How long did you stay? _____

Was it for business or leisure? _____

Did you buy any other travel guides for your trip? _____

If yes, which ones? _____
_____
_____

Thank you for taking the time to complete this questionnaire. Please send it to us as soon as possible, and remember, you do not need a stamp (*unless posted outside the UK*).

AA Travel Insurance call **0800 072 4168** or visit **www.theAA.com**

The information we hold about you will be used to provide the products and services requested and for identification, account administration, analysis, and fraud/loss prevention purposes. More details about how that information is used is in our privacy statement, which you'll find under the heading "Personal Information" in our terms and conditions and on our website: www.theAA.com. Copies are also available from us by post, by contacting the Data Protection Manager at AA, Fanum House, Basing View, Basingstoke, Hampshire RG21 4EA.

We may want to contact you about other products and services provided by us, or our partners (by mail, telephone or email) but please tick the box if you DO NOT wish to hear about such products and services from us by mail, telephone or email. ☐